What Your Colleagues Are

"Understanding what foundational skills are and how to support adolescents is critical in schools today. *Teaching Foundational Skills to Adolescent Readers* provides a much-needed resource for educators to learn how to teach foundational skills to adolescents in engaging and meaningful ways. In this text, Fisher, Frey and colleagues provide insight into adolescents' literacy journeys and demonstrate how theories of effective literacy instruction apply to practice. Readers are provided with examples of how to teach foundational skills explicitly and with flexibility to support a variety of adolescent readers. This text is a must read for teachers as well as for all educational professionals who want to support adolescents' self-efficacy, motivation, and the necessary foundational skills needed to be successful in middle school and beyond."

Margaret Vaughn,
Professor
Washington State University, Pullman, WA

"As a former middle school reading intervention teacher, I wish I'd had access to this book earlier in my career; its insights would have greatly benefited my students and made my teaching practice more impactful and fun. This book will undoubtedly become an indispensable resource for educators looking to enhance their instructional methods and support striving readers. I highly recommend this book to all educators committed to improving literacy outcomes for secondary students."

Ryann Derington,
Staff Development & Curriculum Specialist
Tulare County Office of Education, Visalia, CA

"*Teaching Foundational Skills to Adolescent Readers* is the book secondary educators have been waiting for. I've always known that many of my students struggled with reading, but I was never equipped with the knowledge of literacy or the tools to accelerate my students' learning as readers. This book is unlike any other in that it provides us with the info and skills to make a difference for our students' reading ability, which will in turn allow us to accomplish our mission as secondary educators of setting students up for a brighter future. I cannot wait to use this book to support my teachers and my students."

Emily Brokaw,
Assistant Principal
North Lake Early College High School, Dallas ISD, Dallas, TX

"This thorough guide to adolescent literacy instruction provides educators with a rich array of practical strategies, offering educators a wealth of insights to enhance student learning and achievement. With its clear writing style, relevant examples, and actionable steps, this book is an invaluable resource for both novice and experienced teachers seeking to improve literacy outcomes in their classrooms."

Jenean Bray,
ELA/ELD Curriculum Specialist
Tulare County Office of Education, Visalia, CA

"There is no age limit on learning to read! This fact is even more critical for adolescent students. Students who have been unsuccessful face even greater challenges overcoming reading deficits. The good news is it is never too late to learn. Practitioners must first change their mindset and instructional practices. This book is research rich, providing a solid foundation of critical instructional practices, as well as providing easy-to-implement strategies. A must read for all practitioners!"

Lydia Bagley, Ed. S.,
Instructional Support Specialist/MTSS Coordinator
Cobb County School District, Marietta, GA

TEACHING
FOUNDATIONAL
SKILLS TO
ADOLESCENT
READERS

TEACHING FOUNDATIONAL SKILLS TO ADOLESCENT READERS

Douglas Fisher • Nancy Frey • Sarah Ortega
Kierstan Barbee • Aida Allen-Rotell

Illustrations by Kierstan Barbee

FOR INFORMATION:

Corwin
A SAGE Company
2455 Teller Road
Thousand Oaks, California 91320
(800) 233-9936
www.corwin.com

SAGE Publications Ltd.
1 Oliver's Yard
55 City Road
London EC1Y 1SP
United Kingdom

SAGE Publications India Pvt. Ltd.
Unit No 323-333, Third Floor, F-Block
International Trade Tower Nehru Place
New Delhi 110 019
India

SAGE Publications Asia-Pacific Pte. Ltd.
18 Cross Street #10-10/11/12
China Square Central
Singapore 048423

Vice President and
  Editorial Director: Monica Eckman
Director and Publisher: Lisa Luedecke
Content Development Editor: Sarah Ross
Product Associate: Zachary Vann
Production Editors: Laura Barrett and
    Tori Mirsadjadi
Copy Editor: Shannon Kelly
Typesetter: C&M Digitals (P) Ltd.
Proofreader: Theresa Kay
Indexer: Integra
Cover Designer: Gail Buschman
Marketing Manager: Megan Naidl

Copyright © 2025 by Corwin Press, Inc.

All rights reserved. Except as permitted by U.S. copyright law, no part of this work may be reproduced or distributed in any form or by any means, or stored in a database or retrieval system, without permission in writing from the publisher.

When forms and sample documents appearing in this work are intended for reproduction, they will be marked as such. Reproduction of their use is authorized for educational use by educators, local school sites, and/or noncommercial or nonprofit entities that have purchased the book.

All third-party trademarks referenced or depicted herein are included solely for the purpose of illustration and are the property of their respective owners. Reference to these trademarks in no way indicates any relationship with, or endorsement by, the trademark owner.

Printed in the United States of America

Library of Congress Cataloging-in-Publication Data

Names: Fisher, Douglas, 1965- author. | Frey, Nancy, 1959- author. | Ortega, Sarah, author. | Barbee, Kierstan, author. | Allen-Rotell, Aida, author.

Title: Teaching foundational skills to adolescent readers / Douglas Fisher, Nancy Frey, Sarah Ortega, Kierstan Barbee, Aida Allen-Rotell.

Description: Thousand Oaks, California : Corwin, [2025] | Includes bibliographical references and index. | Summary: "This book delves into the lives of adolescent readers, exploring their struggles and the impact on their academic journey. By utilizing extensive research behind what works best for teaching older students how to read, we propose practical and systematic approaches to address a learner's connection with school and learning"— Provided by publisher.

Identifiers: LCCN 2024041511 | ISBN 9781071926451 (spiral bound ; acid-free paper) | ISBN 9781071972519 (epub) | ISBN 9781071972526 (epub) | ISBN 9781071972533 (pdf)

Subjects: LCSH: Reading (Middle school)—Curricula—United States. | Reading (Secondary)—Curricula—United States. | Reading comprehension—Study and teaching (Middle school) | Reading comprehension—Study and teaching (Secondary) | Literacy—Study and teaching (Middle school) | Literacy—Study and teaching (Secondary) | Teacher effectiveness—United States.

Classification: LCC LB1632 .F574 2025 | DDC 428/.4071273—dc23/eng/20241205
LC record available at https://lccn.loc.gov/2024041511

This book is printed on acid-free paper.

25 26 27 28 29 10 9 8 7 6 5 4 3 2 1

DISCLAIMER: This book may direct you to access third-party content via web links, QR codes, or other scannable technologies, which are provided for your reference by the author(s). Corwin makes no guarantee that such third-party content will be available for your use and encourages you to review the terms and conditions of such third-party content. Corwin takes no responsibility and assumes no liability for your use of any third-party content, nor does Corwin approve, sponsor, endorse, verify, or certify such third-party content.

Contents

List of Videos ix

Publisher's Acknowledgments xi

About the Authors xiii

Introduction: Who Are Adolescent Readers? 1

Chapter 1. Self-Efficacy: Foundational for Adolescent Success 11

Chapter 2. Background Knowledge: From the Known to the New 33

Chapter 3. Word Recognition: Free Up Cognitive Space, One Word at a Time 59

Chapter 4. Word Knowledge: The More You Know, the More You Can Learn 79

Chapter 5. Sentence Analysis: Unlocking the Structure of Language 101

Chapter 6. Verbal Reasoning: Thinking With Words Across Texts 119

Chapter 7. Intervention: Supporting Readers to Develop Automaticity in Word Recognition 141

Coda	167
References	171
Index	179

 Visit the companion website at
**https://companion.corwin.com/courses/
TeachingFoundationalSkills**
for downloadable resources.

Note From the Publisher: The authors have provided video and web content throughout the book that is available to you through QR (quick response) codes. To read a QR code, you must have a smartphone or tablet with a camera. We recommend that you download a QR code reader app that is made specifically for your phone or tablet brand.

Videos may also be accessed at
**https://companion.corwin.com/courses/
TeachingFoundationalSkills**

List of Videos

Chapter 1

Video 1.1: Jigsaw

Video 1.2: Cognitive Barrier Survey Interview

Video 1.3: Value Activity

Chapter 2

Video 2.1: Background Knowledge

Video 2.2: Pre-assessments

Video 2.3: Text Sets

Video 2.4: Search Term

Video 2.5: Advance Organizers

Video 2.6: Short Recap

Video 2.7: Metacognition Self-questioning Interview

Chapter 3

Video 3.1: Fire Science Arm Tapping

Video 3.2: Flexible Word Chunking

Video 3.3: Read This

Video 3.4: Choral Reading

Chapter 4

Video 4.1: Word Knowledge

Video 4.2: Morphology

Video 4.3: Self-Assessment

Video 4.4: Self-assessment Interview

Video 4.5: Routines for Academic Language Concept Sort

Video 4.6: Hexagonal Thinking

Chapter 5

Video 5.1: Juicy Sentences

Video 5.2: Sentence Combining

Video 5.3: Crafty Sentences

Video 5.4: Close Reading

Chapter 6

Video 6.1: Metacognition

Video 6.2: Summarizing

Video 6.3: Visualizing

Video 6.4: Tag the Text

Video 6.5: Scaffolds

Chapter 7

Video 7.1: Reading Assessment

Video 7.2: Scope and Sequence

Video 7.3: Explicit Instruction

Video 7.4: Systematic Instruction

Video 7.5: Fluency Pyramid

In this book, you will be invited into classrooms as teachers engage in authentic work with students. We did not script these lessons, attempting for perfection. Rather, we provide you with real examples of the hard work of teachers who volunteered to allow us into their learning environments.

Publisher's Acknowledgments

Corwin gratefully acknowledges the contributions of the following reviewers:

Jenean Bray
ELA/ELD Curriculum Specialist, Tulare County Office of Education
Visalia, CA

Emily Brokaw
Assistant Principal, North Lake Early College High School, Dallas ISD
Dallas, TX

Heather Casey
Professor, Rider University
Lawrence Township, NJ

Ryann Derington
ELA/ELD Staff Development and Curriculum Specialist, Tulare County Office
of Education
Visalia, CA

Doug Frank
Manager, Reading Language Arts Department, Dallas ISD
Dallas, TX

MaryAnn Suhl
Principal, Alex W. Spence MS & TAG Academy, Dallas ISD
Dallas, TX

We would also like to acknowledge the following individuals who allowed us to record and use content from their classrooms so that you would have examples of quality teaching and learning:

- Betty Collins
- Christopher Nakashima
- Spencer Carroll
- Emily Brokaw
- John Hervey
- Maggie Fallon
- Maria Grant
- Drew Seery
- Nikolina Trgo
- Marnitta George
- Jeff Bonine
- Nick Swift
- Maya Barragan
- Alexandra Prince
- Anna Salazar Moss
- Bethany Crawford
- Matt Trammell
- Sarah Preston

Further, we would like to acknowledge the expert videography skills of Peter Gray and Lacey Kalina.

About the Authors

Douglas Fisher is a professor and chair of educational leadership at San Diego State University and a teacher leader at Health Sciences High and Middle College. Previously, Doug was an early intervention teacher and elementary school educator. He is a credentialed English teacher and administrator in California. In 2022, he was inducted into the Reading Hall of Fame by the Literacy Research Association. He has published numerous articles on reading and literacy, differentiated instruction, and curriculum design, as well as books such as *The Teacher Clarity Playbook, PLC+, Artificial Intelligence Playbook, How Scaffolding Works, Teaching Reading,* and *Teaching Students to Drive Their Learning.*

Nancy Frey is a professor in educational leadership at San Diego State University and a teacher leader at Health Sciences High and Middle College. She is a credentialed special educator, reading specialist, and administrator in California. She is a member of the International Literacy Association's Literacy Research Panel. Her published titles include *How Teams Work, Kids Come in All Languages, The Social-Emotional Learning Playbook,* and *How Feedback Works.*

Sarah Ortega is an accomplished instructional coach, bilingual educator, administrator, and author with deep expertise in supporting multilingual learners and fostering inclusive instructional practices. She has led initiatives as the Coordinator for Instruction and Support for English Learners at Health Sciences High and Middle College and has two decades of classroom teaching experience. In 2023, she was honored as the Chula Vista Elementary School District Teacher of the Year. Her work has been featured in professional development programs and educator publications, showcasing her ability to design high-impact learning experiences. Sarah partners with schools and districts to implement strategies that promote student growth across emotional, behavioral, and academic domains.

Kierstan Barbee holds a doctoral degree in educational leadership and literacy from the University of Houston. She brings almost 20 years of education-related experience in PreK-12 settings. She has served as a secondary English Language Arts teacher, academic coach, and professional development supervisor in urban districts. She most recently served as a project manager of assessment for learning, which involved creating system-wide professional learning programming for central staff and campuses that promoted the spread of research-based practices. Through an emphasis on relationship-building and human-centered design principles, Kierstan has coached PreK-12 principals, teachers, and district leaders on pedagogical practices that promote equity and student agency in learning.

About the Authors

Aida Allen-Rotell is a credentialed bilingual teacher, special educator, and administrator in California. She has served as an academic coach and coordinator of coordinator of services for multilingual learners, and administrator. She led efforts to improve student learning, which resulted in her school earning academic distinction for impacting the lives of students living in poverty, becoming a Visible Learning+ Gold Certified school, and improving academic language for multilingual learners. She also served as an advisor to many high school clubs, was the student government advisor, and led students to championships for 10 years in Health Occupations Students Association (HOSA) competitions.

Introduction
Who Are Adolescent Readers?

The Kid Who Doesn't Try

I don't see what the other kids see

They look at the words on the page

And it means something to them

Their eyes widen

Faces of understanding

Faces of meaning

My eyes hopelessly scan the page

Looking for what they see

But I can't put it together

Desperately disconnected

Unable to see what they all see

—Carlos, Age 15

In this book, we delve into the lives of adolescent readers, exploring their struggles and the impact that reading skills have on their academic journey. We share stories like Carlos's to shed light on the daily battles faced by students who, for various reasons, find it difficult to connect with written words. Educators of adolescents stand at the forefront of a monumental task: teaching content while nurturing the reading skills needed to access that content. And in the meantime, these same educators are often trying to rekindle the joy of learning for those who have lost enthusiasm.

Despite continued dialogue about the importance of literacy and literacy instruction, troubling reading data continue to hang over our nation. The National Assessment of Educational Progress (NAEP) scores for fourth- and eighth-grade students' reading comprehension have been declining, reaching levels lower than those observed in all previous years since 2005 and 1998, respectively (NAEP, 2024). Substantial disparities persist according to race, ethnicity, and socioeconomic status. However, the decline in scores is not limited to students of color or students receiving special education services. Lower-performing scores come from students from a variety of backgrounds (NAEP, 2024).

To make matters worse, secondary school learners with gaps in their reading skills often suffer from insecurities about their capabilities and intelligence, and many have lost confidence in their ability to learn. Some of these students are sitting silently in our classrooms, hoodies up and heads down, trying to disappear into their seats. Others who appear angry and defiant opt for confrontation as a distraction from their academic struggles. Some learners are chronically absent because they are frustrated and failing (Malkus, 2024).

Looking beyond these behaviors, we find students who do not want anyone to discover they cannot pull the words off the page. They are desperately trying to avoid being exposed as students who can't read or who can't read well enough to comprehend their academic texts. These students use a range of strategies to hide the fact that comprehending text is difficult for them. They tend to rely on verbal information—from the teacher and from their peers—to gain content knowledge. Some of these students may get passing grades in their classes, but their relationship with school changes over time. School is less joyful for all learners who are continually compensating for not being able to read well. Thus, secondary teachers are required to teach content aligned with state standards, prepare students for state and national exams, prepare students for higher education and professional life, *and* teach reading skills so students can access the content.

The good news is that it's never too late to learn. From an equity standpoint, we believe that all students can read and read well, and from an empathy standpoint, it is devastating that they can't do so yet. Part of our role as educators is to first overcome this idea of "They should know this by now" and then move into the idea "But they don't know it yet, so I'll teach them."

If we agree that people's values influence their motivation to engage in tasks, then we can conclude that learners need reading proficiency to develop a positive self-concept around reading and the efficacy to tackle more challenging reading. For students to build a positive self-concept about learning, they need small but frequent wins in reading—little mental bursts of satisfaction that come from succeeding in a task that has proven challenging. As educators, how can we design learning experiences that allow students to experience success?

Fortunately, the evidence on the effective literacy components critical to supporting adolescent readers is well documented (Alexander & Fox, 2011; Cantrell et al., 2018; Goldman et al., 2016). But understanding how to approach literacy instruction in secondary classrooms requires more than implementing a set of instructional approaches. Literacy research must be concretely and explicitly connected with the needs of teachers who are experts in their content areas. It also must be connected to a framework that considers the human aspects of learning. To connect literacy research and classroom practice, we will explore the following questions:

- How do middle and high school teachers perceive and understand the challenges faced by struggling readers in their classrooms?
- What approaches can educators use to simultaneously support the acquisition and consolidation of grade-level content and reading skills?
- Which instructional approaches and strategies do secondary teachers consider effective in supporting struggling readers, and how do those perceptions align with existing research and evidence?

Extending What's "Foundational" for Older Readers

There is a common misconception that an eighth-grade student who is assessed at the third-grade level on a measure of reading is able to read like a third-grader making expected progress. But older readers who struggle often possess a profile that is more scattered and uneven in terms of strengths and areas of need. For example, that thirteen-year-old possesses more content knowledge than the eight-year-old does. Or the older student may struggle when decoding multisyllabic words but have a higher-than-expected vocabulary. There is evidence that adult readers who do not possess solid foundational reading skills use the components they *do* have in ways that differ from children (Nanda et al., 2010). Likewise, Tighe and Schatschneider (2014a) found that models of reading development used with typically developing children proved to be a poor fit for adult readers.

The students discussed in this book are not adults, but they are not children either. Some of the approaches used in the early grades, such as attention to decoding, do not have exactly the same effect on older students. A series of four studies with students of different ages is instructive. The researchers provided 125 hours of small group intervention to students of different ages with reading disabilities, focused primarily on phonological awareness and decoding. As shown in Figure i.1, the impact of the intervention on reading comprehension among the second- and third-graders was statistically significant, but there was a decline on the impact on reading comprehension with middle and high school students (Lovett et al., 2022).

Figure i.1 • Effect of Intervention Assignment by Age

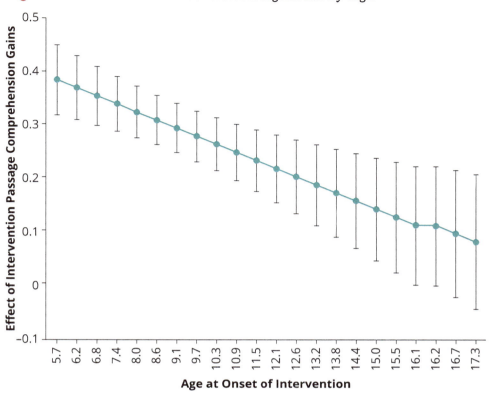

Source: Used with permission of Elsevier Science & Technology Journals, from *Interpreting comprehension outcomes after multiple-component reading intervention for children and adolescents with reading disabilities*, Lovett, M. W., Frijters, J. C., Steinbach, K. A., De Palma, M., Lacerenza, L., Wolf, M., Sevcik, R. A., & Morris, R. D., vol 100, 2022; permission conveyed through Copyright Clearance Center, Inc.

This *should not* be misinterpreted as meaning that developing the foundational reading skills of older students is a wasted effort. To the contrary, the foundational reading skills of phonological awareness, phonics, and fluency have rightly earned the name because they are crucial for older struggling readers to master; nothing replaces them. However, adolescent readers not yet making expected progress need more. They need background knowledge to read. They need stronger verbal reasoning skills to make sense of the logic of textual information and arguments. They must have opportunities across the school day to analyze passages from the level of a single sentence to much longer passages. When these are paired with traditional foundational reading skills, the impact on reading comprehension is amplified. Thus, we argue that foundational reading skills for adolescents include background knowledge, word recognition, word knowledge, sentence fluency, and verbal reasoning. Each of these plays a critical role in ensuring that middle and high school students continue to develop their reading skills as they progress from elementary school to college and career options.

In this book we explore the extensive research behind what works best for teaching older students how to read well. Students with reading abilities that fall below grade level fall into two categories (Archer et al., 2003):

1. Those who can read basic words and have memorized some high-frequency words but struggle with decoding multisyllabic words
2. Those who have unfinished learning in foundational reading skills

We will address the needs of both groups. First, we will consider the needs of the learners who have basic word knowledge. Chapters 2 through 6 are dedicated to classroom practices teachers can use with the whole class or with small groups to integrate reading support seamlessly with content learning. In Chapter 7 we specifically address the requirements of learners who still need to attain or improve foundational reading skills.

Throughout this book we propose practical and systematic approaches to address this critical need and to reimagine a learner's connection with school and learning. Following this introduction, we focus on how secondary educators can align the research with the needs of students in their classrooms. Our goal is twofold:

1. To equip you with the understanding of what might be happening with learners who are not comprehending grade-appropriate texts
2. To provide you with specific knowledge that can help you identify the barriers and design time-efficient, one-on-one strategies to help readers in both whole and small groups.

As we explore solutions to these pressing challenges, let us briefly turn our attention to the structure of this book and how we break down the complex nature of this topic into actionable insights and strategies.

Overview of Chapters and Framework

Let's take a moment to familiarize you with the chapters and features of the book that can support your journey of recharging reading practices for adolescent readers. Figure i.2 illustrates the important concepts of teaching reading to adolescent students; it's also the framework for this book. The energy source is self-efficacy, representing a student's belief in their capabilities. As discussed in this chapter, educators play an important role in developing a student's self-efficacy. That motivation energizes the battery that houses the critical components of reading instruction: background knowledge, word recognition, word knowledge, sentence analysis, and verbal reasoning.

Figure i.2 • A Model for Adolescent Literacy

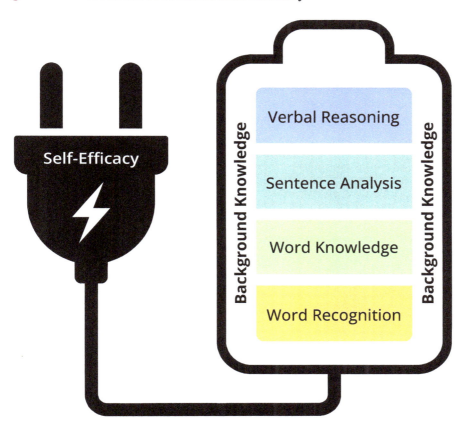

Introduction: Who Are Adolescent Readers? In this introduction we begin to uncover the stories of students like Carlos. We present our understanding of the struggles faced by adolescent readers and the obstacles faced by the educators entrusted with their learning. This section sets the stage for a systematic presentation of the research intertwined with practical application.

Chapter 1. Self-Efficacy: Foundational for Adolescent Success. A holistic approach to adolescent literacy is represented by the connection to the plug labeled as *self-efficacy,* which sets the stage for students' motivation and cognitive engagement. As students gain independence at each of these levels of literacy development, their belief in their own ability to read and comprehend effectively acts as the driving force that powers the entire system. In this chapter we explore the factors that contribute to self-efficacy and the actions that teachers can take to develop students' efficacy.

Chapter 2. Background Knowledge: From the Known to the New. In the illustration of the battery, the concept of background knowledge surrounds word recognition, word knowledge, sentence analysis, and verbal reasoning. It represents the reservoir of knowledge essential for students to connect new information. This chapter explains how prior knowledge contributes to improved comprehension and engagement. It also explores how teachers can activate students' background knowledge, build background knowledge, and teach students to activate their own knowledge to bridge new learning.

Chapter 3. Word Recognition: Free Up Cognitive Space, One Word at a Time. Word recognition is at the base of the battery; it is a foundational component of creating skilled readers, and it is strongly connected to spelling. This stage emphasizes the fundamental ability to decode individual words, especially multisyllabic ones, by understanding how to read units of words rapidly. In this chapter we examine techniques that enable students to read with accuracy and fluency, allowing them to focus more effectively on extracting meaning from the text.

Chapter 4. Word Knowledge: The More You Know, the More You Can Learn. Word knowledge involves recognizing words and understanding their meanings and the nuances. It includes knowledge of the morphemes, affixes, roots, and bases that comprise multisyllabic words. Word knowledge supports students' understanding of both universally important and content-specific vocabulary. For learners, this involves not just knowing a word but also understanding the concepts it represents. In this chapter we explore the research on and practices for word learning and morphological awareness.

Chapter 5. Sentence Analysis: Unlocking the Structure of Language. Sentence analysis focuses on the ability to comprehend and extract meaning from sentences and see the connections between sentences. For students, comprehending within and across sentences is critical to understanding longer texts. Secondary textbooks and articles often contain complex sentences that are syntactically sophisticated. To gain knowledge from texts, readers connect ideas within sentences and across sentences. Sentence-level comprehension is often overlooked in secondary classrooms, but it can serve as a great scaffold to help students understand longer, complex texts.

Chapter 6. Verbal Reasoning: Thinking With Words Across Texts. Students must learn to use the skills they have developed at the word and sentence levels to comprehend longer texts. Understanding the logical flow of ideas is essential in spoken and written language. It's known as *verbal reasoning* because this combination of skills allows for the transformation of ideas and information in the mind of the reader. Students need to be able to make inferences, connect concepts, and evaluate ideas to transfer their learning to new situations. Throughout this process, they are engaging with texts at a deeper level, making

connections from text to text, and thinking critically about the content. This chapter explores how we can help students navigate complex texts and extract meaning from extended passages.

We also would like to emphasize that although the vertical stacking of these components insinuates foundational pieces, it is in no way meant to send the message that students must attain a foundational level of mastery before attending to the other components. On the contrary, instruction and practice is critical for verbal reasoning regardless of a student's current reading proficiency.

Chapter 7. Intervention: Supporting Readers to Develop Automaticity in Word Recognition. The reading strategies outlined in this book are part of quality instruction, but some students will still need supplemental or intensive reading interventions. We might think about this as a secondary source of power, or a supercharger, that fuels the components. This chapter is designed to familiarize classroom teachers with the hallmarks of multicomponent reading intervention (MCRI) programs outside the classroom for adolescents. As members of school organizations, it is crucial for all educators to be informed about evidence-based practices in intervention so they can advocate for and support the work done by interventionists in their schools.

While our primary focus in this book is on strengthening the reading skills of adolescents, at various points throughout the book we also discuss concepts or strategies related to writing and oral language development. Written and spoken language are interconnected and, to some extent, interdependent. It's important to note that although these elements share connections, they each have their own set of processes that require specific direct instruction and practice. Our conceptual framework is designed to promote the development of reading skills so adolescent readers in our classrooms become critical consumers of content knowledge and perhaps even find a love of reading to gain knowledge and enjoyment.

Overview of the Book and Its Features

Throughout the book you will encounter several distinctive features that enhance your reading experience.

- *Plug Into the Research.* Each chapter begins with an overview of the research that underpins the discussion and application of that section of the literacy model.
- *Power Up Classroom Practice.* In these sections we connect the dots of literacy research, classroom practice, and the human aspects of learning.

- *Voices From the Field.* These sections highlight secondary teachers and examine how they have chosen to apply a particular strategy to support grade-appropriate reading and comprehension.
- *Take Charge: Conclusion and Reflective Questions.* Each chapter concludes with key ideas that summarize the essential concepts discussed. These sections also encourage you to reflect on the chapter and consider how you could implement the tools and methods presented in your specific teaching subject or department, or with the students you support.

Thankfully, students have you and other educators like you to help transverse the gap. The job of an educator is not just to see potential but also to

- cultivate it,
- acknowledge the big dreams of students and to excel well past what they think that they can accomplish,
- disrupt the bell curve in education, and
- believe in students who don't yet believe in themselves.

In his convocation speech at the Harvard Graduate School of Education, graduate Donovan Livingston (2016) proclaimed,

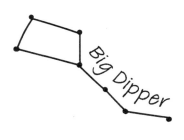

> To educate requires Galileo-like patience.
>
> Today, when I look my students in the eyes, all I see are constellations.
>
> If you take the time to connect the dots,
>
> You can plot the true shape of their genius—
>
> Shining in their darkest hour.

You are the teacher your students have been waiting for. You have the passion and the desire to help students exceed the expectations they have for themselves. Our goal for this book is to help you see how.

CHAPTER 1

Self-Efficacy
Foundational for Adolescent Success

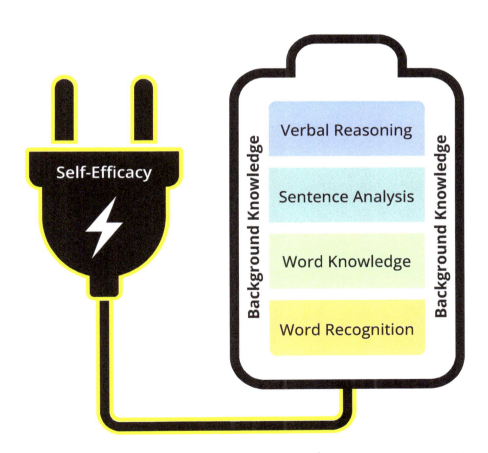

In India, the traditional way of elephant training relies on using a rope to tie a baby elephant's leg to a stake in the ground. Initially, the baby elephant spends days pulling and kicking in a vain attempt to break free. Eventually, the baby elephant realizes the struggle is useless and gives up—to the point

that even when it is fully grown (five thousand to eleven thousand pounds), it no longer fights the rope, even when that rope is tied to a tree the elephant could easily snap. By that point, the elephant has been conditioned to believe that its effort will result in failure (Tracy, 1996). Thus, it doesn't even try.

This passive behavior has been termed *learned helplessness* in the psychology literature (Maier & Seligman, 1976).

As you have probably witnessed, it applies to some of our students as well. You have likely encountered students who put forth very little effort. Perhaps that is because they have developed learned helplessness and believe their efforts will be futile.

Plug Into the Research

We don't want students to feel helpless and hopeless. In fact, academic help-seeking is associated with higher achievement (Fong et al., 2023). Self-efficacy—the belief that we have the wherewithal to accomplish our goals—is crucial for learning and for self-regulation, including help-seeking (Bandura, 1977; Hole & Crozier, 2007). In general, people who have higher levels of self-efficacy experience more work satisfaction and less distress and anxiety about the tasks they must complete. For the classroom, our framework highlights how self-efficacy charges the components needed for secondary reading instruction. In fact, it is a crucial component for all learning processes (Cantor et al., 2019). Consequently, helping students build self-efficacy is a critical aspect in fostering adolescent literacy (Alexander & Fox, 2011; Wolters et al., 2014).

There are several things educators must do to build students' self-efficacy. First, they need to help students set a learning goal. What does the student want to accomplish? Goal-setting is a critical aspect of building efficacy. Students who do not have goals have significantly reduced efficacy and actually accomplish less than those who do have goals, in part because they do not devote the required effort needed to meet specific intentions (He et al., 2023). Of course, the solution is not for educators to tell students what their goals should be; rather, teachers should support learners with goal-setting tasks. For students, ownership of the goal is as important as understanding why it is worthy of attention.

Second, efficacy requires students to believe they have what it takes to accomplish the goal. In essence, at times we all ask ourselves, "Do I have the skills, the will, and the resources to accomplish this goal?" In the classroom, the answers to these questions should also guide the support that teachers need to provide to students.

Here it's important to note that skills are different from resources, which is different from motivation. Providing a learning experience to someone who already has the skills but lacks motivation is not likely to have an impact. However, providing a learning experience to someone who needs skill-building can make a difference (Bassi et al., 2007). If we analyze what our students need to learn or to receive to be able to accomplish their goals—and then we ensure they develop or receive it—we're likely to increase their efficacy. Motivation as an instructional target is sometimes overlooked, at our own peril. In a reading intervention for middle school students, those who received instruction designed to promote motivation, along with foundational skills instruction, made significantly greater gains in word-reading speed, fluency, and comprehension, compared with students who received only the skills instruction (Lovett et al., 2021).

Third, it's essential to recognize that for learners, self-efficacy is stifled by the absence of success. When students experience success by accomplishing their goal or by making progress toward that goal, their efficacy grows. Unfortunately, too many students fail to recognize the many successes they have achieved. Thus, it is also worthwhile to help students identify and celebrate their accomplishments along the way.

For learners, **success leads to motivation and engagement**, which we will discuss in the remainder of this chapter. For now, know that you can help students develop their sense of efficacy. The good news is that efficacy is situational, developing when it is nurtured (Hole & Crozier, 2007); it's not a personality trait or an inherent characteristic that only some people have. This means you can be that nurturer and increase your students' self-efficacy and, in doing so, elevate their motivation to learn.

Estimates show that motivation accounts for up to 30 percent of application and transfer of learning in adults and adolescents (Colquitt et al., 2000). However, despite its large potential to influence learning, motivation is not necessarily the cause of achievement but rather an outcome (Csikszentmihalyi, 1990). Further, it can be engineered into secondary instruction (Shernoff et al., 2003). Self-efficacy, attribution of success to effort (rather than ability), perceived value of the task, and emotions all contribute to whether students are willing to engage and what level of mental effort they're willing to exert (Clark & Saxberg, 2018). These psychological aspects are influenced by the complexity of tasks, past experiences of success and failure, interests, learning environment, and relationships.

When students experience academic success, they're more likely to engage in behaviors that led to that success (Weiner, 1985). A large study of challenge-seeking and growth mindset among nearly fifteen thousand adolescents in two countries found exactly that (Rege et al., 2021). There's something motivating about tackling a challenge, struggling a bit, and coming out a winner on the other side. When learners experience success, it feeds their motivation to continue, and they want to obtain that feeling again.

Conversely, there's something inherently unmotivating about repeated failure when learners don't get the incremental wins for which they strive. When students experience academic failure and attribute that failure to their own internal abilities, it initiates a vicious cycle of underachievement (Kirschner & Hendrick, 2020). Learners with poor reading ability don't enjoy it, so they read less. When they read less, they don't get better at reading because they are not engaged in sufficient practice for the instruction to stick. In the meantime, more-proficient classmates make further gains in part because of their higher reading volume. This phenomenon has been termed the Matthew effect, echoing the biblical story that "the rich get richer while the poor get poorer" (Stanovich, 1986). Consequently, negative emotions—including guilt, shame, and anxiety—as well as task-avoidant behaviors arise for these students, while their self-efficacy and motivation decrease. Then the cycle continues.

Studies of motivation suggest the one thing that influences motivation more than anything else is success. Students persist in activities where they experience success and avoid with passion those activities in which they're not successful or believe they cannot be (Pintrich, 2003).

To illustrate, let's look at the video game market. Players start a game at its most basic level. Maybe it takes a few tries, but then users achieve the level and move on to the next. Their sense of efficacy grows as they win, and they learn what moves to make next so they can win again. The players' self-efficacy fuels their motivation to continue engaging. Despite the increased difficulty, the video game market has figured out how to balance the right amount of success and challenge to keep users coming back. Constant success is not the motivating factor; frequent incremental success balanced with failure is (Atkinson, 1957; Jeno et al., 2023).

In our classrooms, efficacy, motivation, and engagement must connect in an intricate web to encourage students to initiate, persist in, and exert mental effort in learning.

If learners in our classrooms do not experience success, it's unlikely that many will continue to engage with challenging tasks, particularly reading. It's not fun to fail; it's even less fun to consistently fail. As educators, **we need to create opportunities for students to experience quick wins to build their efficacy with learning**. Whether we're fostering word consciousness or building fluency, it's important to design lessons so all learners experience success. Ultimately, we want to create those lightbulb moments for students that provide mental snaps of satisfaction, which increase learner motivation.

Increase Your Battery Life

There is a lot to know about building student motivation and self-efficacy, but here are some important approaches to consider:

- **Help students become aware of their level of engagement and how it impacts their learning and the learning of others.** When you spend time helping students understand how their effort and engagement matter in learning, you encourage ownership in the classroom.

- **Design lessons with the Goldilocks principle in mind.** Lessons should be not too hard and not too easy—they should be "just right" so students can optimize failure and success (Hattie, 2023). Some lessons and students require scaffolds to access complex texts, and we will focus on various scaffolds in the chapters that follow.

- **Call attention to behaviors that lead to success so students attribute their success to their engagement and effort.** Name successful moves students make when they experience success, such as, "I noticed you intentionally made connections with your background knowledge to help you make sense of this text."

- **Empathize with failure and task avoidance, but don't let disengagement become the norm.** It is easy to see how the negative views students hold about themselves could trigger apathy, social withdrawal, task avoidance, disengagement, or disruptive behavior. Combine caring with high expectations and confidence in their abilities—a teaching characteristic referred to as being a "warm demander" (Sandilos et al., 2017).

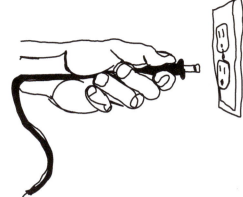

Power Up Classroom Practice

Let's apply research on motivation and self-efficacy to instructional practices that support students' access to content. Here are the classroom practices we will explore:

- Teaching levels of engagement through the jigsaw protocol
- Understanding cognitive barriers to engagement and learning
- Understanding what students value as a means to increase motivation and efficacy
- Mental effort check-ins to monitor students' self-regulation

Classroom Practice: Teaching Levels of Engagement Through the Jigsaw Protocol

We argue that self-regulation and engagement should be taught in the classroom as explicitly as word decoding, writing, or content knowledge is taught. Think about the planning and designing a science teacher engages in when developing a unit on the systems of the body. In a lesson about the digestive system and normal regulation of blood sugar, a science teacher has thought carefully about the visuals, examples, vocabulary, direct instruction, and collaborative work needed to support student understanding. Similar processes should occur when we are teaching learners about student engagement, which occurs along a continuum. As Table 1.1 shows, students can be actively engaged or actively disengaged.

Video 1.1
Jigsaw
qrs.ly/eafya26
To read a QR code, you must have a smartphone or tablet with a camera. We recommend that you download a QR code reader app that is made specifically for your phone or tablet brand.

CHAPTER 1 • Self-Efficacy

Table 1.1 • Continuum of Engagement

ACTIVE		PASSIVE		ACTIVE	
Disrupting	**Avoiding**	**Withdrawing**	**Participating**	**Investing**	**Driving**
• stopping learning • distracting others • making loud or quiet interruptions	• avoiding learning • not being physically present • looking for ways to get out of the work	• mentally separating from the work • daydreaming • not working with the group	• turning in assignments • answering questions • following directions	• asking questions • feeling like the learning is important • thinking of how the learning connects to other ideas	• setting goals • seeking feedback • making self-assessments
Disengagement			**Engagement**		

Source: Adapted from Berry, A. (2022).

Have you ever procrastinated completing a difficult task? Or has your mind ever wandered during a professional learning session? As educators, we need to help students understand that we have all experienced different levels of engagement depending on various factors—and that it's important to be aware of our engagement level. One way to address this in the classroom is through the use of the jigsaw reading technique, a collaborative protocol designed to empower students to serve as experts in a specific dimension of a topic and to prompt them to rely on each other for a more complete understanding of the topic.

Several research studies on the jigsaw reading technique from around the world have reported its positive impact on reading comprehension (Baneng, 2020; Hattie, 2023; Hidayati & Rohayati, 2017; Namaziandost et al., 2020). In this technique, students work with classmates as part of an "expert group." With this group, they work to specialize in their topic in preparation for teaching their fellow students from their "home group." Within their home groups, students depend on the other members to give them insights into the other dimensions of the topic they didn't study. This strategic approach proves beneficial throughout the school year as students are acquiring, consolidating, and working for deeper understanding of various topics. The resulting interdependence not only supports content knowledge acquisition and communication skills but also fosters collective efficacy as students engage in shared learning experiences.

The following instructions show how teachers can use the jigsaw reading technique to help learners understand the different levels of student engagement.

steps for implementation

1. **Assign home groups.** The teacher forms home groups of four to six students.

2. **Divide expert group subcategories.** The teacher assigns each student in the home group to become an expert in one of the following engagement categories: disrupting, avoiding, withdrawing, participating, investing, and driving.

3. **Allow students to become the experts.** Students meet with their expert groups (the other students assigned the same category) to read and analyze the text related to their assigned engagement level. Table 1.2 shows sample texts students could analyze. They discuss and agree on two to four key points that describe their assigned engagement level. They also discuss examples they will share back with their home groups to make the category more visible and comprehensible. Based on teacher preference and time available, there are several aids students could use to convey information, such as posters, digital presentations, skits, or other methods.

4. **Ask students to teach and learn.** Students meet with their home groups and take turns teaching their category they prepared for. Learners use a graphic organizer, like the one in Table 1.3, to take notes and process the information from each group.

5. **Encourage reflection.** After the teaching sessions, students reconvene with their expert groups and debrief the jigsaw process and consider additional insights after their teaching experience. Sample reflection questions include the following:

   - How well do you think you were able to communicate the key points about your assigned engagement category?
   - What went well during your presentation, and what would you do differently?
   - Were there any confusions or misconceptions? How did you help others understand the information?

CHAPTER 1 • Self-Efficacy

Table 1.2 • Six Text Selections for the Jigsaw Protocol for Each Level of Engagement

Disrupting

Imagine this: You're in class, trying to focus on the lesson, but there are some classmates who are not really tuned into the lesson. They're doing things that show they are not into the learning of that day—maybe even cracking jokes, being a bit too loud, or doing things that distract everyone.

Disruptions don't just occur when someone is intentionally trying to disrupt learning. A disruption happens any time the flow of learning gets interrupted. For example, maybe you are following along with the math strategy the teacher is introducing and suddenly there is an announcement over the loudspeaker. That counts as a disruption because there is a temporary stoppage of learning. And it takes a while to get back into the groove of learning.

Quiet disruptions exist too. Imagine you are getting some feedback from a peer on your essay and someone innocently walks up and asks for a pencil. No harm is intended, but again, it takes a moment to refocus your brain.

So, disruptions can be noisy or subtle, intentional or unintentional. But all disruptions mean a temporary halt in the learning for both the disrupter and those being disrupted. You can think of a disruption like a small pebble thrown into a pond. The pebble can cause a ripple effect that impacts the tranquility of the water. It takes a while for that water to settle back to how it was.

Avoiding

Have you found yourself leaving class for a restroom break to avoid doing some work? Some students occupy themselves with tasks like unnecessary restroom breaks, organizing their materials, checking social media, or waiting for help. Often these actions signal that the student is trying to avoid learning.

Avoiding can be a result of big emotions or challenges. When learning feels overwhelming or confusing, students might avoid the work because the challenge feels uncomfortable. Sometimes a person might even avoid a hard task by working on an easier task. Sometimes it is helpful to get a smaller task accomplished before tackling the harder task, but it is important to recognize when you deliberately avoid a particular task so you can make the decision to refocus or to ask for help. What do you think the difference is between taking a break and avoiding work?

The most extreme form of avoiding learning is when students don't show up to class at all. This is a significant problem in education right now. There are many reasons a student might be absent, but we need to figure out why some students decide not to come to school. We should pay attention to how students feel and to the atmosphere in the classroom. It's important for students and schools to recognize when students are avoiding learning and figure out how to change that behavior.

Withdrawing

Think about it: Our brains can't stay focused on learning new information every second of the day. When we are learning, it is totally natural for our minds to drift off to other thoughts and ideas. What do you think about when you daydream or explore other thoughts in your mind?

Although it is natural for our brains to wander from the learning in front of us, being withdrawn involves a little more than getting wrapped up in a momentary thought. We can withdraw in two ways: physically or mentally. Physically withdrawing might look like sinking into your seat during your group's collaboration time or physically stepping away from the learning happening in front of you. The good news is you are not stopping anyone from learning. But you are missing out on the learning. And your group is missing out on the valuable contributions you make.

Mentally withdrawing means that you are not connecting to the learning. You are not physically leaving, but you are not really engaged with what's happening around you either. If you check out for too long, it can get really challenging to dive back into the learning.

It's important to think of the reasons that you are withdrawing from the learning. Confronting the reasons can help you stay focused. Remember, reaching out for help to talk things through with someone can make a big difference. Don't let the learning pass you by. Instead, find strategies to reorient yourself with the learning that's happening.

Participating

If you are doing your work in class, paying attention, and even answering the teacher's questions, how engaged do you think you are? How would you rate your level of engagement? Do those actions make you a stellar student? Would the teacher expect more from you, or are you doing enough?

Let's explore the participation level of engagement. Let's understand what participation is and what it is not. In addition to paying attention and doing the work, participation also means you are coming to school and passing your classes. At this level of engagement, you have started to be engaged in your learning. But notice the key word: *started*. That's because participation falls under the idea of passive learning. Participation is passive learning because while you are following the classroom or school's directions, you are not in control of your learning journey. Think about it like you are in the passenger seat of a car—you are along for the ride, but you are not in the driver's seat.

Should participation be rewarded and seen as the ultimate goal of school?

Investing

Picture this: In math class you are learning about percentages and ratios. You think to yourself, *"When am I ever going to use this in real life?"* Then you land your first job and see that percentages and ratios are everywhere. Your uncle even shares some wisdom with you. He says to save at least 15 percent of your earnings. Suddenly, math isn't just numbers on a page. It applies to real life. Even the math that isn't seen in everyday life is helpful because it helps you develop other skills, like critical thinking. That is what it means to invest in your learning—feeling that it matters. It's important.

Investing in your learning also means that you are not just listening to the teacher but that you ask questions. You ask questions to clarify information, to learn more about a topic, or to check your own understanding. So, when your horticulture teacher is discussing the techniques of grafting plants and you are understanding the process but are not sure why someone would want to do this, you ask. You raise your hand and ask, "What are the benefits of grafting plants?" That is being invested in your learning. Asking questions is a key part of being successful in school and in life.

Driving

Driving your learning is not just about completing tasks and paying attention; it's about being in the driver's seat of your learning journey. Students who drive their learning go beyond the basics.

Students who drive their learning set personal goals aligned with what the class aims to achieve. First, you have to know what the learning goal is for the lesson. Then you can set a goal, such as this one: "Today I am going to ask questions to help me understand the purpose of the figurative language. I'm going to ask people to explain to me how they were able to figure out the meaning of figurative language. Also, I want to add more evidence to my informative essay."

Students who drive their learning set goals, but they also seek feedback so they can get closer to those goals. A student might say, "Can you give me feedback on whether my evidence aligns with my claim?"

And it doesn't end there. Students at this level do not wait for a grade to let them know how they are doing in their classes. They self-assess. They use the criteria or rubrics for the class to monitor their own progress.

Students who are at the driving level of engagement recognize that receiving an education means something. They also seize opportunities to teach others. They want to teach others for two reasons. One is that they enjoy helping their classmates, because learning is supposed to be hard, and we all need help in different areas. But also, they want to teach others, because they recognize that teaching others helps them solidify their own understanding.

Table 1.3 • Expert Group Graphic Organizer for the Engagement Jigsaw

EXPERT GROUP NOTES FOR LEVELS OF ENGAGEMENT			
SUBTOPICS	DESCRIPTION	EXAMPLES	Potential Reasons or Causes for Being on This Level
Disrupting			
Avoiding			
Withdrawing			
Participating			
Investing			
Driving			

Personal Reflection

1. In this classroom, what do you think your typical level of engagement is?

_____

_____

_____

2. Why do you think that is? _____

_____

_____

_____

CHAPTER 1 • Self-Efficacy

3. What would you have to do to move one level up from your typical level?

_____

_____

_____

online resources This resource is available for download at https://companion.corwin.com/courses/TeachingFoundationalSkills.

Notice the personal reflection questions provided in the final step of the jigsaw protocol and located at the bottom of Table 1.3. Students need to reflect on how the recent learning applies to them personally, self-assess their level of engagement, understand why it may vary, and determine how to progress along the continuum of engagement to levels that are more conducive to reaching their goals. Prompt students to check in with their levels frequently. Once you know the amount of effort students put into learning, you can tailor the material or psychosocial interventions to help them with content or to build their confidence accordingly.

Classroom Practice: Understanding Cognitive Barriers Survey

Often educators find that students who enter middle school or high school and struggle academically have difficulty expressing why they have had varied success with school. Sometimes students may be hesitant to express their concerns. In addressing this issue, we draw upon the work of Stephen Chew and William Cerbin (2021), who conducted a systematic review of the existing research literature on student disengagement and identified nine cognitive barriers to learning. They describe a cognitive barrier as "a characteristic or aspect of mental processing that can affect the success or failure of learning" (p. 3). Utilizing their insights, teachers can facilitate conversations with students by presenting a series of statements designed to help them articulate their feelings and experiences. Table 1.4 provides a list of the cognitive barriers to learning.

Table 1.5 provides a list of statements you can share with your students to help them identify the specific cognitive barrier they might be facing. This tool also helps teachers identify the reasons for learning challenges and disengagement, which will then allow you to take action to invite your students back into learning.

Video 1.2 Cognitive Barrier Survey Interview qrs.ly/rffya3s

Table 1.4 • Cognitive Barriers to Learning

CHALLENGE	DESCRIPTION
1. Student mental mindset	• Students hold attitudes and beliefs about a course or topic, such as how interesting or valuable it will be and how capable they are to master it through their own efforts. • Students may believe that a course is irrelevant to them or that they lack the ability needed to learn the content.
2. Metacognition and self-regulation	• Students monitor and judge their level of understanding of concepts, and they regulate their learning behaviors to achieve a desired level of mastery. • Students may be overconfident in their level of understanding.
3. Student fear and mistrust	• Students come to a course with a certain level of fear of taking it. Students may interpret the teacher's behavior as being unfair or unsupportive of their learning, resulting in a certain degree of mistrust. • Negative emotional reactions, such as fear or lack of trust in the teacher, can undermine motivation and interfere with learning.
4. Insufficient prior knowledge	• Students vary in how much they know about course content at the start of the course. • Some students may have little to no knowledge about the content, putting them at a disadvantage compared to students with a strong background.
5. Misconceptions	• Students often hold faulty or mistaken beliefs about the course content at the start of the course. • Students may cling to misconceptions even when taught accurate information.
6. Ineffective learning strategies	• Students can employ various methods to learn course concepts, and these methods vary widely in effectiveness and efficiency. • Students often prefer the least effective learning strategies.
7. Transfer of learning	• Students can vary in their ability and propensity to apply course concepts appropriately outside the classroom context. • Students often fail to apply knowledge beyond the end of a course.
8. Constraints of selective attention	• Students can focus their awareness on only a limited portion of the environment, missing anything outside that focus. • Learners mistakenly believe they can multitask, switching attention back and forth among different tasks.
9. Constraints of mental effort and working memory	• Students have two major limitations in cognitive processing: the amount of mental effort or concentration available to them and the ability to hold information consciously. • Students are easily overwhelmed by trying to concentrate on too complex a task or to remember too much information.

Source: Adapted from Chew, S. L., & Cerbin, W. J. (2020).

CHAPTER 1 • Self-Efficacy

Table 1.5 • Student Interview to Identify Specific Barriers to Engagement

	"Here are some statements that students think about. I'm going to read you a sentence and you tell me if you think that way often, sometimes, or rarely."	OFTEN	SOMETIMES	RARELY
1.	I wonder, "Why do I need to learn this?"			
2.	I don't know how to do the work.			
3.	I'm not really good at school.			
4.	I already know how to do the work; I don't really need to pay attention.			
5.	It's hard to focus in class because I don't feel comfortable asking questions when I'm confused.			
6.	I'm trying, but I don't understand the work.			
7.	I study, but I still don't do well on the tests.			
8.	I think I've learned something, but then I can't do the work on my own.			
9.	I have a hard time paying attention.			
10.	There is a lot of information to remember, and it's hard to remember so many things.			
11.	I use my phone during class, but I think I can still do my work at the same time.			
12.	When I'm doing my work, I get confused or lost.			
13.	I don't think my teachers really like me.			
14.	I notice that my understanding of a topic is different from the information being presented in class.			

This resource is available for download at https://companion.corwin.com/courses/TeachingFoundationalSkills.

Table 1.6 aligns the survey questions to Chew and Cerbin's nine cognitive barriers to learning (2020), and it provides approaches for how you can address each one.

Table 1.6 • Survey Statements Aligned With Cognitive Barriers

COGNITIVE BARRIER DESCRIPTION	QUESTION FROM SURVEY	POTENTIAL APPROACHES
1. Student mental mindset	Question 1, Question 3	Explain the value and importance of the learning, increase students' ownership of their learning, and explore the habits of minds and mindsets.
2. Metacognition and self-regulation (they may be overconfident about their knowledge or skills and therefore they don't devote attention to it)	Question 4	Create reflection assignments; teach students about planning, monitoring, and adjusting their learning; and use practice tests.
3. Student fear and mistrust	Question 5, Question 13	Focus on teacher credibility, restructure feedback, and create a safe climate for learning and making mistakes.
4. Insufficient prior knowledge	Question 2, Question 6	Use initial assessments, provide the lesson's background knowledge and key vocabulary in advance, and use interactive videos.
5. Misconceptions	Question 14	Use advance organizers, recognize common misconceptions for students at a specific age or in a specific content area, and invite students to justify their responses to that thinking.
6. Ineffective learning strategies	Question 7	Teach study skills, model effective strategies with think-alouds, and use spaced practice.
7. Transfer of learning	Question 8, Question 12	Plan appropriate tasks, model application in different contexts, and tailor feedback to include processing of the task.
8. Constraints of selective attention	Question 9, Question 11	Increase teacher clarity, use breaks and reorientation strategies, and teach students to avoid multitasking, especially with media.
9. Constraints of mental effort and working memory	Question 10, Question 12	Organize information and chunk it, use both visual and auditory cues (dual coding), and use retrieval practice.

Classroom Practice: Understanding What Students Value

As teachers aiming to foster the self-efficacy of adolescents, we must acknowledge and support our students' identity and sense of belonging. Belonging isn't just about students fitting into an established organization; it also involves understanding that the organization is continually shaped and reshaped by the students who enter the building. This process can't be left to chance; rather, we need to purposefully cultivate classroom experiences and interactions that affirm our students' personal and academic identities.

Video 1.3
Value Activity
qrs.ly/jffya40

A good start is to understand the values of each of our students—values that have been shaped through their culture, family, and personal experiences. However, some students may find it challenging to spontaneously share their core values. So, a practical activity involves providing students with a list of potential values they can consider, such as the list in Table 1.7.

Table 1.7 • Values

honesty	loyalty	optimism	courage	generosity
success	empathy	kindness	independence	teamwork
knowledge	boldness	spirituality	patience	patriotism
confidence	making a difference	being the best	justice	persistence
fame	power	cleanliness	problem-solving	risk-taking
creativity	humor	harmony	friendships	community
leadership	learning	faith	health consciousness	equity

When we understand a student's values, we can leverage those values to promote stronger social, emotional, and academic identities. Once our students have reflected on the values most important to them, we can choose from many extension activities to help them deepen their thinking around their values. For example, teachers can use the following questions as part of class discussions, independent writing activities, or identity presentations:

- Which values are most important to you?
- Where do your values come from?
- What do your friends, classmates, and loved ones consider to be a value you embody?
- What values are important to you in your friends?
- Can you provide specific examples from your life where your actions aligned with the values you've identified as important to you?
- Can you provide specific examples from your life where your actions did not align with the values you've identified as important to you?
- Why would it be helpful to understand someone else's core values?
- Why would it be helpful for other people to understand your values?
- How can embracing your core values help you positively impact the way you interact with others?
- What is one thing you would need to change to live out your values?
- How does knowing your values help you live a more authentic life?

These questions can help learners articulate their values more thoughtfully when they are communicating their identity with their teachers and peers. Then, by leveraging the students' core values, we can promote stronger social, emotional, and academic identities. This approach creates a more inclusive learning experience, which sets the stage for a meaningful education.

Classroom Practice: Mental Effort Check-In

Middle and high school students are learning to strengthen their self-regulation skills, which is their ability to manage their own actions. The amount of mental effort it takes learners to complete a task or achieve a goal is one measure of their self-regulation (Van Gog et al., 2012). Prompting our students to help them develop an awareness about the role of their mental effort (Dweck, 2007) is key to helping them interrupt a negative fixed mindset (e.g., "I'm not smart enough to understand this reading") and transform it into a growth mindset (e.g., "This reading is challenging but I can persist"). Consider asking students the question shown in Figure 1.1 to check in with their effort after they read a challenging text.

Figure 1.1 • A Measure of Mental Effort

How much effort did you invest to complete the reading task?					
1	2	3	4	5
No effort		Moderate effort		Extreme effort

Source: Adapted from Van Gog et al. (2012).

CHAPTER 1 • Self-Efficacy

Asking students to assess how much effort they applied to complete a particular task can be telling. Students who succeed with low effort are unchallenged; students who succeed with high effort attribute success to effort. Students who do poorly on an assignment and exert no effort versus extreme effort might need a different course of action. Students with low effort may have a low efficacy and need some psychosocial support to engage; students with high effort may need a reteach or an intervention.

Voices From the Field

A group of ninth-grade students took a class inventory involving ten questions about their learning, habits, future plans, perceptions, strengths, and weaknesses. Consider the student responses shown in Table 1.8.

Table 1.8 • Responses to a Class Inventory

WHAT I WANT MY TEACHER TO KNOW ABOUT ME	MY AREAS OF WEAKNESS IN ENGLISH CLASS
I don't get it the first time.	Everything
I need stuff step by step and I learn slow.	Reading i be stuttering when i read i be nervous
I actually am trying just reading is difficult for me.	Don't finish reading on time.
I hate reading out loud in front of other students.	I struggle to understand things and I struggle with pronouncing words and spelling.
I am a slow learner so it might take me a little bit to get stuff figured out.	Reading out loud/spelling
I may need a little extra help.	Comprehension skills
I am going to need more examples to learn.	My weakness in English is reading.
I give up fast but just need a push.	Reading comprehension and writing
I get stressed and mad when I don't understand things.	This is my worse subject. Im not good in this class.
I like to speak in private so I can understand better.	Remembering what I read right after I read it or when im reading im not actually reading something is going thru my head
I am not very good at English.	Reading out loud/spelling
I try my hardest.	I get anxiety when I have to read out loud.
I didn't go to 6th grade so I might be behind.	Reading aloud

Do these students seem like kids who don't care about school? Do they seem like they are unmotivated or unwilling to learn? No. How many of your students would identify with these statements? By the time students reach middle and high school, many have developed negative identities about themselves as learners: slow learner, poor reader, struggling student. Notice the number of students who think learning is supposed to be easy, who think needing help or extra time is a mark of shame, or who believe that struggle is a sign of weakness.

Struggle is situational; it's not an identifier or a label we should cast on students. Our role is to foster positive academic identities where students see themselves as mathematicians, historians, authors, analysts, entrepreneurs, and scientists. But how do we help shape these identities when students don't yet see themselves as belonging in the world of academics?

These same students who self-reported weakness in reading, writing, vocabulary, and learning also responded to another statement: "I want to earn my high school diploma so/because . . ." Their responses appear in Table 1.9.

Table 1.9 • Responses About Earning a Diploma

I WANT TO EARN MY HIGH SCHOOL DIPLOMA SO/BECAUSE . . .	
I want to go to college and be a sportscaster.	I want to be successful when I grow up.
If you don't have one people think you're dumb.	I want to have a good job, and it can help me go to college.
I want to get a good job and have a good life.	I can get a good job and be able to do something I want to do.
I want to be a travel nurse.	I want to be successful and go to college.
It's important because it opens up jobs and college.	I want to make my mom proud. I want to make my family proud.
I want to go to college and do something with my future.	I want to go to music school.

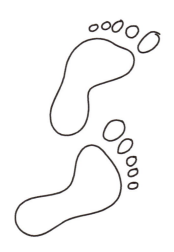

Did you hear it? Despite their self-proclaimed difficulty in learning, they still have big dreams for themselves. A 2018 study by The New Teacher Project (TNPT) had similar findings: Ninety-four percent of students surveyed in diverse urban, rural, and charter districts aspired to attend college, and 70 percent of high school students in the survey had career goals that required at least a college degree. Our goal as educators is to help students meet and exceed the goals and potential they have for themselves. Once we understand how they view themselves, we can be the catalyst that accelerates their journey.

Take Charge: Conclusion and Reflective Questions

Educators can consider the psychological aspects of efficacy, motivation, and engagement in the context of student learning. Little, satisfying wins—like the ones players experience in video games—can energize students to search out more of those wins. The Goldilocks principle suggests that designing lessons with the right amount of challenge can optimize the learning experience by providing students with the energy that comes with succeeding on a challenge.

We recognize that cognitive barriers to learning can hinder academic progress, but understanding and then addressing our students' specific barriers can help learners feel valued and supported in achieving goals.

Choose one of these questions to reflect on your practice and take charge to support learning for all students:

- Think about the experiences of students who have struggled to connect with school. How can you show students that their unique identities and values are integral to their classroom community?

- Consider the depth in which you plan and design content lessons. How can you explicitly teach students about their level of engagement with the same intentionality?
- Reflect on the importance of shaping positive academic identities for students. In what ways can you encourage a classroom culture that views struggle as situational rather than as a permanent identifier?
- Consider the importance of quick wins in fostering motivation. Think of an upcoming learning experience you've planned. How can you design for quick wins so all students experience academic success?

CHAPTER 2

Background Knowledge
From the Known to the New

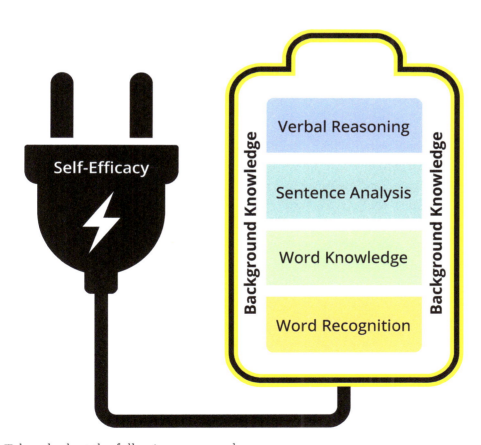

Take a look at the following paragraph:

> The intricate cascade of neurotransmission commences with the depolarization of presynaptic membranes, culminating in the exocytotic release of neurotransmitter-laden vesicles into the synaptic cleft,

where they engage with their cognate receptors on the postsynaptic membrane, thus catalyzing receptor-mediated ionic fluxes that underpin the generation of excitatory or inhibitory postsynaptic potentials. This sophisticated molecular dance is tightly regulated by re-uptake transporters, enzymatic degradation, and autoreceptor feedback mechanisms, imparting exquisite spatiotemporal precision to neurotransmitter action, thereby governing the fine-tuned orchestration of cognitive, sensory, and motor processes in the intricate tapestry of neural function. (OpenAI, 2024)

Could you visualize it? Were you able to make inferences? When you reread the text, did it give you any more insight about the main idea? Were you able to create synthesis across the text to explain the topic? Maybe. If you used your knowledge of word parts, perhaps you were able to understand some pieces, but without background knowledge, your general reading comprehension strategies likely did little to help you create meaning.

Plug Into the Research

Background knowledge is the network of information we all use to make meaning while we listen and read. It is the "knowledge relevant to the text under study" (Brody, 2001, p. 241).

Cognitive science indicates students learn new ideas by connecting them to previous knowledge; new information that is not otherwise anchored gets discarded (Hattie & Yates, 2014). In students with sufficient background knowledge already in place, their subsequent learning gains are not strongly tied to the knowledge they already possess and instruction works to improve their learning. But for students with little existing background knowledge to draw upon, their ability to make learning gains from instruction is severely compromised. Simonsmeier and colleagues (2022) performed a meta-analysis of 493 studies about prior knowledge to test the "knowledge is power" (KIP) maxim in education. Surprisingly, they found that KIP was more nuanced. They provided this example: For students who already possess sound number sense in math, their prior knowledge is not especially predicative of how much they will learn about how to add fractions. But a classmate who does not have a good grasp of number sense will likely struggle with the content. They offer a knowledge threshold hypothesis that provides more distinction to KIP:

> The threshold hypothesis implies that prior knowledge correlates more strongly with knowledge gains in participants with below-average

amounts of prior knowledge because some of these learners might still lack knowledge that is indispensable for learning. Conversely, in learners with above-average amounts of prior knowledge, the correlation between prior knowledge and knowledge gains would be low or zero, because these learners have all the prior knowledge they need to learn effectively. (p. 47)

As another example, if you haven't reached the knowledge threshold about neurochemistry needed to understand the opening paragraph of this chapter, it is more difficult to benefit from the information, let alone draw conclusions and pose deep questions.

For students not yet making sufficient progress in reading, knowledge is power when it comes to surpassing the knowledge threshold. Specifically, **background knowledge greatly influences students' ability to comprehend, think critically, and draw conclusions in texts**. When students' background knowledge is strong, they can more readily comprehend complex texts because as they read they're able to fill in missing or incomplete information about a topic that the author assumed readers know (Ozuru et al., 2009). Conversely, when students' background knowledge is lacking, comprehension can suffer even for the most motivated readers because they have more difficulty making the logical leaps necessary to fill in the blanks (Elbro & Buch-Iversen, 2013).

By activating and building our students' background knowledge, we can significantly aid their reading comprehension efforts. Many studies have demonstrated the impact of background knowledge on adolescent readers (Hattan & Alexander, 2021; Kintsch, 1998; McCarthy et al., 2018; Tarchi, 2010). One seminal study by Recht and Leslie (1988), commonly called "the baseball study," illustrated the impact of background knowledge on seventh graders. The results showed that when poor readers had background knowledge on baseball, they performed at similar levels to otherwise strong readers who lacked background knowledge on baseball.

A more recent meta-analysis (Filderman et al., 2022), which examined sixty-four studies focused on identifying effective comprehension interventions for students from third to twelfth grade, confirmed that background knowledge plays a significant role in reading comprehension and has a substantial impact on reading outcomes. This influence was evident across all grade levels studied, but it was particularly pronounced among secondary students.

But why does background knowledge influence comprehension, particularly for middle and high school students? It's because **the more learners know, the more efficiently they absorb and comprehend new information**. Now pair this knowledge with what we know about the school texts adolescents are required to read. In secondary classrooms, discipline-specific texts and topics grow increasingly more complex and nuanced; thus, as students progress through grade levels, the amount of background knowledge they are required to have in order to be able to comprehend texts successfully increases.

As educators, knowing what background knowledge our students possess helps us know the appropriate knowledge we need to foster for a lesson. Activating and building our students' background knowledge primes their understanding of new disciplinary content. The more exposure learners have with a topic, the deeper their knowledge base about the topic grows. Further, the more their knowledge grows, the more critically they can think, because their comprehension and their access to their existing knowledge expands.

Make Background Knowledge Useful

For background knowledge to be useful, learners must be able to locate it and then apply it. This sounds straightforward, but this statement masks the complexities that have vexed teachers through time. A teenager's closet is a good analogy here. Many of us have had experiences with sending an adolescent to their room to retrieve an item—say, a backpack. In this case you know they own the backpack because you paid for it yourself.

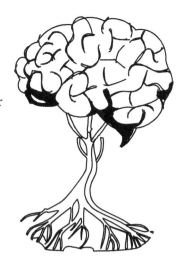

But whether that teenager can locate the backpack in the closet is another matter altogether. Further, there may be an issue of motivation: Despite your request, the teenager may not be invested in finding the backpack. Or the problem may be that the closet, which holds the backpack, is completely disorganized. On the other hand, the issue may not be organization but rather knowing *when* the item is needed. Even though the backpack is required for school every day and it's easy to locate, perhaps the teenager simply never gets it unless you prompt them. They know where it is, but for some reason they aren't conditionalized to know *when* they'll need it.

It's also possible that this learner shows the same tendencies at school—they leave their belongings behind in classrooms, and they rarely arrive at a new activity with the tools they need to complete the task. In this case, the learner is not transferring from one situation to the next, especially when there are new activities. The inability to use one or more of these factors—knowing where to find their tools or knowledge, knowing when they need those tools or that knowledge, knowing how to use both in a new situation, or wanting to have knowledge and tools available—interferes with their performance. In other words, possession alone isn't enough.

The National Research Council's report titled *How People Learn: Brain, Mind, Experience, and School* (2000) describes a framework for understanding how background knowledge supports new learning:

> The new science of learning does not deny that facts are important for thinking and problem solving.... However, the research also shows clearly that "usable knowledge" is not the same as a mere list of disconnected facts. Experts' knowledge is connected and organized around important concepts (e.g., Newton's second law of motion); it is "conditionalized" to specify the contexts in which it is applicable; it supports understanding and transfer (to other contexts) rather than only the ability to remember. (p. 11)

Background knowledge in learning is like the shutter on a camera lens. Just as the shutter controls how much light enters the camera to create a clear image, background knowledge that is organized, conditionalized, and transferable influences how much new information a student can effectively take in and understand. Without the right amount of light, a picture can be blurry or too dark. Similarly, without sufficient background knowledge, new information might be confusing or overwhelming. The shutter needs to be adjusted according to the light conditions, just as teaching needs to be tailored to build on what students already know, ensuring they have a clear and comprehensive understanding of new concepts (see Figure 2.1). These three concepts—*organized, conditionalized,* and *transferable knowledge*—ensure that background knowledgeable is useable. Let's look more closely at the evidence for each.

Figure 2.1 • Making Background Knowledge Useable

Organized

Schema theory lies at the heart of the first provision necessary for background knowledge to be useful (McVee et al., 2005). A schema represents a hierarchical representation of knowledge, connected to other related information. For example, your knowledge of pizza includes its characteristics (food, round, dough, red sauce), types of pizza (cheese, vegetarian, pepperoni), and pizzas that don't fit all the characteristics (square pan, BBQ chicken). In addition, your schema for pizza is connected to other schema (food, sports events, restaurants, Italy). Rumelhart (1984) described the characteristics of schemas as representative of knowledge (rather than isolated facts), nested within other schema, variable, and acted upon by the learner.

Your useable knowledge of pizza is easy for you to retrieve because it is organized and connected to other facts. An important factor in your ability to maintain this organizational structure is that it is clustered around a big idea rather than simply a bunch of isolated facts. In contrast, consider a topic that may not be well organized in your mind (perhaps opera, car engines, or rugby). In any of these cases, if you are not an expert or have not developed an organizational structure, you might be able to come up with a few facts (e.g., *Carmen* is an opera), and you might even be able to link them (e.g., operas, like car engines and rugby, are noisy), but that's about it. Unfortunately, this isn't good for learning.

However, a learner who possesses a schema for knowledge can draw upon it in much more sophisticated ways. You may have a great deal of knowledge about operas or car engines or rugby, which is influenced by your prior experiences and your interest. For our students, essential

Video 2.1
Background
Knowledge
qrs.ly/tnfya42

prior experiences include those that occurred both inside and outside the classroom. Therefore, as teachers, when we organize new knowledge in ways that support the development of schema, we are making it possible for our students to find it in their mental closet. The National Research Council notes,

> Expert teachers know the structure of their disciplines, and this knowledge provides them with cognitive roadmaps that guide the assignments they give students, the assessments they use to gauge students' progress, and the questions they ask in the give and take of classroom life. In short, their knowledge of the discipline and their knowledge of pedagogy interact. (2000, p. 155)

Our students' experience with learning plays a role as well. As adolescents engage with more formal disciplines during the middle and high school years, they are required to assimilate knowledge into increasingly more complex schemas. Here again, your role as the teacher plays an important part in this equation. Students can benefit from teachers providing organizational aids such as notetaking tools and graphic organizers precisely because they mirror the mental models they should be constructing (Williams & Eggert, 2002).

For example, in a unit of study on plants, tenth-grader Ashley's teacher activated her background knowledge about cellular structure to foster an understanding of the similarities and differences between plant and animal cells. The teacher provided students with organizational schema for living things, and Ashley was able to use that knowledge and apply it to plants. As she explained, "All living things must be capable of homeostasis, organization, metabolism, growth, adaptation, response to stimuli, and reproduction. I'm organizing my notes by these seven factors because I know they all have to be present because plants are living things."

Conditionalized

The second factor necessary for background knowledge to be useable is that it must be conditionalized. That is, the learner must know where and when to apply it. Remember the scenario of the teenager who knows where the backpack is but never seems to remember to get it when preparing to leave the house for school.

That adolescent is not yet conditionalized. And yes, part of conditionalized learning relates to motivation. If your students are motivated, then they are more likely to apply what they know almost automatically. That said, we're not speaking so much of behavioral conditioning as we are of the decision-making that goes on in a learner's head as they decide what background knowledge they should apply. Rumelhart (1984) characterized schema as being nested within other schema, an argument in support of the practice of fostering connections across knowledge bases and disciplines, in order to better conditionalize knowledge.

We were reminded of this while observing a ninth-grade English teacher during a think-aloud based on the short story "Kipling and I" by Jesús Colón (1961). As part of her think-aloud, she identified relevant background knowledge and noted why this was important.
In her words,

> I don't know why he has to read by the light from the streetlamp. Oh, but now I remember the pictures I found of New York at the turn of the 20th century. Lots of people didn't have electricity. They thought life would be better by immigrating to the U.S., but it wasn't. They were poor and often couldn't afford electricity. So now this makes sense; he's reading by the streetlight because he doesn't have his own light in his apartment.

With that one think-aloud, the teacher demonstrated how her brain clicked through related schemas to call forth the information she needed to understand a text's detail.

Another useful image to consider is that while all the background knowledge of the world is vast, it's still an ordered universe when you look at it arranged into disciplines. And within these disciplines, there are hierarchies of information and concepts. Consider, for example, the stance held by some science educators that physics should precede biology and chemistry (Bardeen & Lederman, 1998). They assert that physics principles govern other scientific concepts, such as osmosis in biology, or molecular structures in chemistry.

Others disagree. Sadler and Tai (2007) performed a large-scale study of eight thousand college students and found that sequence did not predict grades in introductory science courses, but the number of years of high school mathematics did. While the best sequence for high school science education is debatable, both camps recognize the critical role that background knowledge plays in acquisition of new learning. Sophisticated schema of physics and mathematics appears to be associated with higher levels of science learning (Sadler & Tai, 2007). In other words, students' ability to connect background information, in this case mathematics with science, is important for their achievement. When they are missing information or only have bits and pieces of disconnected information, learning is interrupted.

The inability to apply background knowledge can interfere with the kind of deep analysis adolescent learners are required to perform. And that's where teachers come in. We have to constantly guide students in developing and activating relevant background knowledge, and we need to assist them in suppressing what is not useful.

As educators, we witness this "right church, wrong pew" phenomenon in classrooms frequently. For example, a group of eighth-grade students were analyzing fables to determine the moral of the story. One of the groups was assigned "The Tortoise and the Hare." In their discussion, a student named Andrew shared his background knowledge about turtles. He said,

> I know a lot about turtles. They're cold-blooded and live on every continent, except Antarctica. Turtles have pretty good eyesight and a really good sense of smell. Their shell even contains nerve endings so they can feel things on their shell. They're one of the oldest kinds of reptiles and have outlived other species that have gone extinct. Their breeding cycle is complicated, but all turtles lay eggs on the land.

While correct and interesting, the background knowledge that Andrew activated won't help him analyze the moral of the fable his group was assigned. In fact, his thinking about this information might even interfere with his ability to analyze the text. He's thinking about the biological world, while the assignment requires that he think about the metaphorical world. Having said that, you can probably guess that Andrew understands that tortoises, which are a subgroup of turtles, are generally considered slow movers. And that tiny bit of background knowledge would probably be of more help for this unit on fables than his considerable knowledge of the species.

Transferable

As previously noted, students must possess an organized schema of knowledge, and they must utilize it appropriately to understand new information. The third condition for learning as described by the National Research Council is that students must also transfer background knowledge to novel situations. Of course, transfer is dependent on good first teaching, without which transfer isn't possible. As a reader, you might be engaged in transfer in this chapter as you have applied the familiar metaphor of the teenager's backpack to help you reach a new understanding for this framework for learning.

Transfer, which is the *application* of new learning, is always a chief goal of our teaching. It's kind of why we set alarm clocks and get to school each morning, hoping that our students will take all the footballs of knowledge we've tossed their way and run with them into their lives. But let's be honest—it's one of the biggest challenges we face each day. We have found ourselves on more than one occasion bemoaning the fact that we modeled and demonstrated how to do something in our courses and gave students lots of opportunities to replicate it, but when it came time for our students to use what they knew in a novel situation, they struggled.

The research on establishing subgoals has been very helpful in our own teaching practices to promote transfer. Establishing subgoals with students involves chunking the steps necessary to complete a task (e.g., Margulieux & Catrambone, 2021). Think of it as organizing minischemas. The evidence suggests that novices have difficulty transferring background knowledge to novel situations because they attempt to memorize a sequence rather than pay attention to the conceptual aspects of the task (Atkinson et al., 2003). When the steps are grouped into conceptually similar chunks, transfer improves.

This was demonstrated in a study of 112 statistics students who were taught about two types of statistical hypothesis tests (*t*-tests and ANOVA), using either a model that emphasized computational steps or one that emphasized conceptual ones. Although both groups performed similarly when asked to read and solve equations closely matched to the ones done in class (the *t*-test problems), the students taught under the conceptual condition were able to apply their skills at a higher level when faced with novel situations that did not closely replicate what they had done in the classroom (the ANOVA problems) (Atkinson et al., 2003). There is research evidence that knowledge is transferred in pieces, not as a wholly formed abstract concept (Wagner, 2010).

For example, in Casey Rossi's twelfth-grade science class, her students learned a great deal about geology and the difficulty of planetary investigations. They also studied robotics, mechanics, and data collection. While the unit was conceptually rigorous, the students in this class, some of whom were reading below grade level, had opportunities throughout the course to regularly engage with projects that provided opportunities to transfer what they had been learning through application of authentic problems.

For example, Ms. Rossi created a culminating project for this unit that required students to transfer their understanding. Their assignment was to build a planetary explorer that gathered the type of data they needed to describe this previously unknown place. Each team built a computer-controlled rover that collected the information they wanted to analyze. Students maneuvered their rovers into one of several four-foot cubes covered with sheeting. Using optical cameras on the rover, the student teams could view the landscape inside the cube. They used robotically controlled arms to collect soil and rock samples. The planetary rovers also included measurement instruments for gauging temperature and humidity to determine whether water might be present. After guiding the rover out of the unknown planetary space, the teams then had to assemble the data and analyze it to make predictions with supporting evidence about the space's composition and characteristics. By creating a project that emphasized conceptual knowledge rather than the completion of a defined set of steps, Ms. Rossi gave her students, including those reading below grade level, an opportunity to transfer their background knowledge to a new situation.

Increase Your Battery Life

There is a lot to know about activating and building background knowledge, but here are some important approaches to consider:

- **Activate and, when necessary, build background knowledge.** If students don't have adequate background knowledge, they have nothing for new information to "stick" to, and therefore their learning breaks down. Take time to understand what your students already know. This will help you build the bridge to what they need to know to be successful in your classroom.

- **Check-in with knowledge.** Identify what prior knowledge your students have and don't have through preassessments or quick polls. Don't make assumptions about what students know and don't know.
- **Act on it.** Once you've identified what knowledge your students bring to the table, use that information to guide your planning and teaching. Make explicit connections between what the students know and what you want them to know.

- **Be wary of providing too much background knowledge up front.** This is a tricky balance. Our tendency is to tell students all things immediately to eliminate their struggle or to skip the need for them to do additional reading altogether. Struggle is okay. Decide on the knowledge students need to know going into the lesson, then use an analogy or an advanced organizer as a bridge to new content.
- **Mix it up.** Choose a variety of ways to activate and deepen your students' background knowledge throughout the course of the semester so students have different ways to showcase their current level of understanding in low stakes, not-for-a-grade ways.

Power Up Classroom Practice

Let's apply research on background knowledge to instructional practices that support students' access to content. Here are the classroom practices we will explore:

- Activating Prior Knowledge
  - Initial assessments
  - Language charts
  - Anticipation guides
- Building Background Knowledge
  - Text sets
  - Targeted search terms
  - Advance organizers
  - Short recaps
- Teaching Students to Activate Background Knowledge
  - Self-questioning
  - Mark my confusion

Classroom Practice: Activating Prior Knowledge

Activating prior knowledge refers to the strategies teachers use to surface students' prior knowledge on topics for which they may have previous learning. Teachers aim to help learners establish connections between their existing knowledge and newly introduced concepts. There are several ways to activate prior knowledge, such as through the use of preassessments or having students complete tasks and engage in discussions.

Initial Assessments

Initial assessments are low-stakes ways to see what students already know. Open-ended questions, quizzes, and polls give teachers quick insight into what students already know about an upcoming unit. For a more informal approach, preview the unit or lesson goal(s) and ask students what words and phrases they already know in the goal, which words and phrases they've heard before but don't know, and which terms or concepts they are unfamiliar with. Figure 2.2 provides an example of a low-stakes initial assessment.

Video 2.2
Pre-assessments
qrs.ly/ctfya46

Figure 2.2 • Example of a Low-Stakes Initial Assessment

1	2	3	4	5
I've never heard of this.	I've heard it but I'm not sure what it means.	I can tell you a little bit about it.	I can explain several facts about it.	I can teach my class about this.
Electromagnetic energy				
1	2	3	4	5
Electrical energy				
1	2	3	4	5
Mechanical energy				
1	2	3	4	5
Thermal energy				
1	2	3	4	5

Language Charts

Record your students' thinking on a poster paper, a whiteboard, or an online form to activate what they already know. One tool for this approach is a K-W-L chart. K-W-L (know-want-learn) is a three-step inquiry process for reading instruction designed to unearth students' background knowledge about what they *know*, identify what they *want* to know, and consolidate their knowledge through what they've *learned* at the end of a lesson (Ogle, 1986). Importantly, this process promotes critical and reflective thinking. Teachers can utilize a three-column K-W-L chart in online platforms like Pear Deck, Nearpod, or FigJam, or they can use analog options like chart paper or whiteboards with sticky notes. The point is that your students discuss and record their responses to each of the three questions and in doing so they activate their background knowledge.

K-W-L has also been adapted to include other cognitive tasks through the following letters:

- **H:** How can I learn more? (Ogle, 1986)
- **S:** What do I still need to learn? (Moore et al., 2000)
- **U:** How will I use what I've learned?

CHAPTER 2 • Background Knowledge

Consider the adaption from The National Behaviour Support Service (n.d.) in Table 2.1.

Table 2.1 • K-W-L-U Chart for Reading

K	W	L	U
What we think we KNOW now	What we WANT (or need) to learn	What we LEARNED	How we will USE what we learned
Before you read		**While** you read	
		After you read	

Source: Adapted from The National Behaviour Support Service (n.d.).

Another unique spin on K-W-L is Think, Puzzle, Explore from Project Zero (Ritchhart & Church, 2020). This thinking routine invites students to write what they *think* they know about a topic, what *puzzles* or questions they have about the topic, and what they're excited to *explore* about a topic. Using this protocol, you can unearth your students' misconceptions as they explain their preconceptions and background knowledge about the topic of study.

Having said that, adolescents can be reluctant to name what they want to learn (the second question). They may be concerned with what peers will say if they express they don't know something. One way to overcome this potential barrier is to consider relevancy in learning. As teachers, *we* know why we what them to learn information and concepts. But students may not see how these are relevant to their lives. Make sure to articulate *why* the upcoming unit is relevant to them. In addition, model how your own intellectual curiosity is sparked by the upcoming content.

You can use a technique called Hooks and Bridges to do so (Silver et al., 2018). The "hook" is used to capture students' interest (e.g., "Have you noticed that there are lots of stories in the media about what billionaires are doing and wearing?") and is used to spur some initial discussion and invite them to consider the value or importance of the topic. Follow it by the "bridge" to your unit. Sixth-grade social studies teacher Jess Alvarado posed that hook, then bridged during a K-W-L about the ancient Roman Empire: "Did you know Roman emperor Augustus Caesar may have been the richest man in history? It's estimated that he was worth the equivalent of $4.6 trillion in today's money. He ruled the ancient Roman Empire for forty-five years. What questions does that cause you to consider about what life was like for different members of society at that time?"

Anticipation Guides

Anticipation guides are pre- and postorganizers that function in two ways: They give students a preview of the concepts and themes they will encounter in a unit or text, and they assess students' prior knowledge, understanding, and beliefs. Teachers organize anticipation guides using true/false statements or agree/disagree statements both before learning and after learning has taken place.

True/false anticipation guides provide educators with an early understanding about the existing knowledge or misconceptions students have about factual topics. When you are teaching more ambiguous topics, you can use anticipation guides to activate your students' prior knowledge by having

learners agree or disagree with key themes or concepts related to a reading and explain their reasons to their peers. As students read the text, they can qualify or challenge their previously held beliefs with new information acquired in their reading. The continued exposure helps your students acquire the necessary knowledge.

Table 2.2 provides an example of an anticipation guide for social studies. The statement in the center allows students to agree or disagree both before and after reading. As an extension, students can provide evidence on a few statements that affirm or justify their opinions after reading.

CHAPTER 2 • Background Knowledge   49

Table 2.2 • Sample Social Studies Anticipation Guide

BEFORE READING THE TEXT		STATEMENT	AFTER READING THE TEXT		
AGREE	DISAGREE		AGREE	DISAGREE	EVIDENCE
		1. If a country holds elections, they have a functioning democracy.			
		2. Government policies have a minimal impact on the day-to-day lives of citizens.			
		3. Laws are inherently morally right.			
		4. Democracy is on the decline worldwide.			
		5. Democracy ensures equal economic opportunities for everyone.			
		6. Civic engagement ends at voting.			
		7. Democracy has an equal chance of being established and maintained in any country regardless of history or culture.			
		8. Democracy cannot be manipulated by external forces.			
		9. The United States actively promotes the rise of democracy solely for ideological reasons.			

Video 2.3
Text Sets
qrs.ly/fcfya49

Classroom Practice: Building Background Knowledge

To build our students' background knowledge, we must intentionally provide learners with new information and experiences that expand their knowledge base on a specific topic. Ultimately, what learners understand and what they pay attention to is determined by their ability to build background knowledge, activate it, and pair it with prior experiences.

Quad Text Sets

Text sets use multiple texts and text types to build and deepen students' knowledge and language comprehension around a particular theme, topic, or essential question. One version of text sets is a quad text set (Lupo et al., 2020). Unlike conventional text sets, which are designed to provide information about a topic, quad text sets draw on a variety of text modalities and complexities to build knowledge, motivation, and linguistic access. This includes digital texts, especially those that are multimodal. In addition, they are used to move from more readily accessible texts to provide entry into a topic to increasingly complex texts that draw on the initially constructed background knowledge.

- *Multimodal texts* build knowledge visually. Short videos, graphic novels, sketch notes, advertisements, interactive maps, images, and virtual reality experiences are all examples of multimodal texts that can help build knowledge.

- *Accessible informational texts* build knowledge. Choose texts that are accessible to students. The material should convey an entry-point level of informational knowledge you want students to acquire.

- *Motivational texts* build interest. Choose texts that lead to the excitement of exploring a topic or concept in more detail.

- *Texts that are more complex* allow students to apply their growing content knowledge. Once students have developed a general understanding of a topic, choose a more challenging text that dives deeper into the content but is anchored to concepts explored in the former texts. Again, the goal is to develop learners' background knowledge so students can connect prior knowledge to help organize new knowledge. Table 2.3 shows an example of the quad text framework, developed by eighth-grade teacher Rhonda Phillips for her unit on overcoming obstacles.

CHAPTER 2 • Background Knowledge

Table 2.3 • Example of a Quad Text in Eighth-Grade English

MULTIMODAL TEXTS		INFORMATIONAL TEXTS	
Selected Text	**Instructional Mode**	**Selected Text**	**Instructional Mode**
Video: "The Pencil's Tale" (https://www.youtube.com/watch?v=HisYsqqszq0)	Whole class viewing and discussion	Excerpt from *A Long Walk to Freedom* (Mandela, 1994) "Lessons From Failure: Why We Try, Try Again" (Brookshire, 2015) Excerpts from *Fantastic Failures* (Reynolds, 2018) on Seabiscuit, Ilhan Omar, and Luis Fernando Cruz	Teacher-directed whole class and reciprocal teaching groups
MOTIVATIONAL TEXTS		**CHALLENGE TEXTS**	
Selected Text	**Instructional Mode**	**Selected Text**	**Instructional Mode**
Out of the Dust (Hess, 1997) *A Long Walk to Water* (Park, 2010) *Rez Dogs* (Bruchac, 2021)	Student-directed literature circles	"To Build a Fire" (London, 1908) "Girl" (Kincaid, 1983) "Civil Peace" (Achebe, 1971)	Teacher-directed close readings with text-based questions and extended discussion

The decision to use motivational and multimodal texts functions as a scaffold that helps students access more complex texts. In doing so, background knowledge is built and then used to understand increasingly complex texts.

Targeted Search Term

Another way to help students build their own quick background knowledge and integrate technology is to give them five minutes to find out as much information on a topic as they can. After time is up, they can compare their notes with a partner's notes and add or amend to create a deeper understanding of a topic. This gives students quick access to information in a constrained time crunch, and it also gets students talking about the topic to create another touchpoint for internalizing the information. In order to avoid choice fatigue or to enhance the validity of the research, teachers can also point students to a given website or websites and then allow them to choose which information they find important, relevant, or intriguing.

Video 2.4
Search Term
qrs.ly/g9fya4c

Video 2.5
Advance Organizers
qrs.ly/mffya4e

Advance Organizers

An advance organizer is a textual or visual framework a teacher presents to the class in advance of the lesson to help form the basis for what students will be learning (Ausubel, 1968). These short texts or visuals are designed to structure information for students so they have a high-level overview of what they're about to learn. They are not graphic organizers for students to complete but rather serve as a map of how major concepts are linked. Here is a list of some of the different organizers teachers can use to help students gain some familiarity:

- *Expository.* Describes new knowledge a learner will need to understand; relates information to what is already known.
- *Narrative.* Presents information in a story format to activate background knowledge to help learners connect to new information.
- *Skimming.* Provides a high-level overview that focuses on titles, headings, and subheadings before reading the material more carefully.
- *Graphic.* Offers pictographs, concept maps, and descriptive visuals or patterns to overview the information that will be explored.

The goal of advance organizers is not to give away the learning up front but to provide learners with a generalized preview of the content to be read and learned. To help students bridge the gap between new and prior learning, use familiar concepts and vocabulary anchored to the soon-to-be-learned concepts. For example, seventh-grade science teacher Bennett Randolph created an advance organizer for his students to use at the beginning of a unit on cells (see Table 2.4).

Table 2.4 • Advance Organizer for Cell Unit

Three Concepts About Cell Theory

All living organisms are composed of cells.

The cell is the basic unit of life.

All cells arise from preexisting cells.

FEATURE	ANIMAL CELL	PLANT CELL
Cell membrane	Yes	Yes
Cell wall	No	Yes
Nucleus	Yes	Yes
Cytoplasm	Yes	Yes
Mitochondria	Yes	Yes
Chloroplasts	No	Yes
Vacuole	Small or none	Large central vacuole
Lysosomes	Yes	Rarely
Centrioles	Yes	No (present in lower plants)

Video 2.6
Short Recap
qrs.ly/5xfya4g

Short Recaps

Review is an important part of learning; it helps students form stronger connections to material and improves the ease of access for which they can subsequently retrieve or recall previously learned concepts. As an integral piece of effective instruction, psychologist Barak Rosenshine (2012) suggests a short recap (five minutes) to help students consolidate previously learned material, get a preview of new concepts and terminology, and make connections to the new learning. Consider using the following practices during daily review (Rosenshine, 2012, p. 13):

- Review the concepts and skills that were practiced.
- Ask students about concepts where they had difficulties or made errors.
- Review material where most errors were made.
- Review material that needs overlearning (i.e., newly acquired skills should be practiced well beyond the point of initial mastery, leading to automaticity).

Through short recaps we can help our students activate their previous knowledge to consolidate their learning and build explicit connections to new learning.

Classroom Practice: Teaching Students to Activate Background Knowledge

Activated background knowledge serves well as a comprehension strategy; dormant background knowledge does not. While teachers can assist in building learners' background knowledge, it's essential for students to learn how to activate this knowledge independently.

Self-Questioning

When students independently read a text, there are questions they can ask themselves before, during, and after reading. These questions can help them activate what they already know about a topic or help them identify where

Video 2.7
Metacognition
Self-Questioning
Interview
qrs.ly/trfya4j

they have gaps in understanding. Table 2.5 contains examples of questions teachers can encourage students to use to question their thinking and understanding.

Table 2.5 • Teaching Students to Self-Question

PLANNING FOR LEARNING BEFORE READING	MONITORING LEARNING DURING READING	REFLECTING ON LEARNING AFTER READING
What information on this topic do I already know?	What is the most confusing thing about this information? Where am I getting stuck?	What decisions did I make to get unstuck in my learning?

Mark My Confusion

Reading with a pen in hand is one way to keep learners accountable to a text. When we ask students to pay attention to the concepts or places in a text that are confusing, it allows us to see where their comprehension is getting muddy. It's also an exercise in metacognition (thinking about one's thinking), because students are actively paying attention to what is making sense and what is still unclear (Flavell, 1979). Students can mark sentences that are confusing, words or concepts they don't know, or paragraphs that are a bit fuzzy. With this approach, students help us pinpoint where their comprehension is breaking down. Learners can either continue reading for additional clarification and revisit the confusing parts or they can ask the teacher to help them with the text.

Voices From the Field

To activate and consolidate knowledge about topics related to the American Revolution, eleventh-grade U.S. history teacher Emily Brokaw utilized a K-W-L (see Figure 2.3). This allowed students to think about what they already knew about the topic of the lesson, pose their own questions, and reflect on their learning at the end of the lesson. As a result of the knowledge gleaned, Ms. Brokaw was able to quickly reinforce the background knowledge students came to the table with and determine where she needed to spend more time teaching. She was also able to better design upcoming lessons to

CHAPTER 2 • Background Knowledge

build from what students knew to make decisions about what primary and secondary sources students needed to deepen knowledge around unfamiliar topics.

Using the quad text set framework, tenth-grade English teacher Luis Borrego selected the texts shown in Table 2.6 to deepen his students' knowledge of the author's craft and understand the complexities of injustice. In addition, he identified how students would engage with the readings.

Table 2.6 • Mr. Borrego's Quad Text Set

MULTIMODAL TEXTS		INFORMATIONAL TEXTS	
Selected Text	**Instructional Mode**	**Selected Text**	**Instructional Mode**
Excerpts from *Maus II: A Survivor's Tale: And Here My Troubles Began* by Art Spiegelman	Students move through stations containing different excerpts to build background knowledge	Selected chapters from *The Sunflower: On the Possibilities and Limits of Forgiveness* by Simon Wiesenthal	Jigsaw
MOTIVATIONAL TEXTS		**CHALLENGE TEXT**	
Selected Text	**Instructional Mode**	**Selected Text**	**Instructional Mode**
"Lamb to the Slaughter" by Roald Dahl	Partner-read to hook students on the complexities of injustice	Excerpt from *12 Years a Slave* by Solomon Northrup	Close reading with modeled think-alouds before release

In this case, Mr. Borrego's use of text sets also contributed to the students' general language development for noticing patterns of injustice and how authors intentionally craft language to impact the logic and emotions of readers. By using a quad text selection of engaging and thought-provoking texts, he ensured that his students were exposed to the complexities of language and essential ideas that learners need so they can successfully read challenging texts.

Teaching Foundational Skills to Adolescent Readers

Figure 2.3 • K-W-L Responses in a History Class

American Revolution K-W-L

What do I KNOW about the American Revolution?

What I know is that the American revolution was an epic political and military struggle —Yullanra Hernandez

Exchanged gunfire at Lexington and Concord in Massachusetts

I know that one of the main causes of the American Revolution, was the boston tea party and coercive acts

I know that The American Revolution also called the U.S. War of independence— was the insurrection fought between 1775 and 1783. —Kassandra g

I Know that the American Revolution was about America fighting for independence —Adriana V

I know that during the American Revolution they jailed colonist who refused to participate the war until they agreed to join. —Diana G.

What I know is that during the American revolution war they used rhetoric to convince large numbers of working class colonists to fight against Great Britain

I Know that it occurred in colonial North America, 1765–1979

I Know America wanted Independence. —Andrea J

American revolution involved a fight between the colonist and the Britains and American wanted to claim independence from them and were struggling. —Joshr.

I know the American Revolution began in North Carolina —Juan A

The American Revolution was when America was fighting for independence from Great Britain. An early battle was the battle of Lexington —Alondra Maldonado

What I know about the American Revolution is that they were doing what they believed right "no taxation without representation". —Stephanie Nunez

The Founding Fathers won the Revolutionary War in large part because they convinced large numbers of working class colonists to fight against Britain. —Romina C

I Know that it was America claiming independence from Britain. America got tired of how they didn't get full control over what happened next . . . —Dayna Sifuentes

All I know about the American Revolution that it was a political war. —Chris. R.

I know that one of the main reasons tocause the American Revolution was the Boston tea party, and the coercive acts

I lean that it gave rise to the first civil rights movement and resulted in the first large–scale constructions of free black life.

What do I WANT TO KNOW about the American Revolution?

I want to know how the British colonies rebelled against the rule of Great Britain —Yullanna Hernandez

How was Great Britain affected afterwards? —Alondra Maldonado

I want to know what type of effect it had towards other colonies or towards Great Britain

I would like to know how America beat the British —Stephanie Nunez

I want to know how did the American Revolution effected the GB after the war had ended. —Diana G.

I want to know the main cause of the American Revolution. —Juan A.

I want to know why they called it the American revolution —Kassandra g.

What I want to know about the American Revolution is if it affected the perspective of the government's power.

I want to know what was the main thing that helped Americans win the revolution. —Adriana V

What were the effects for everyone

What effects did the war have? —Andrea J

I want to learn a little more in dept between thoughts of American and Britain. —Josh r.

What was the main event that caused the American Revolution? —Dayna Sifuentes

CHAPTER 2 • Background Knowledge

What have I LEARNED about the American Revolution?

I learned that the American Revolution were successful because they got help from the French.
—Diana G.

I know they rejected the imperial rule

I learned that it lasted from 1775 until 1783
—Yulianna Hernandez

I Learned that the Boston tea party was trigger for the American Revolution.
—Stephanie Nunez

I learned that the American revolution caused many conflicts towards Great Britain.

I learned that only five people died in the Boston Massacre

It was caused by the bad treatment that Britain would give the colonies. Also, that it inspired the French Revolution.
—Dayna Sifuentes

American Revolution was successful
—Andrea J

How did the Stamp Act Congress pave the road for American independence?
—Kassandra g.

I learned that a large portion of colonists were either neutral or supported the kilnd during the American Revolution militia because they believed it would lbring them fortune –Adriana V

American revolution was able to move forward because they received support from the French.
—Josh r.

Credit: Emily Brokaw

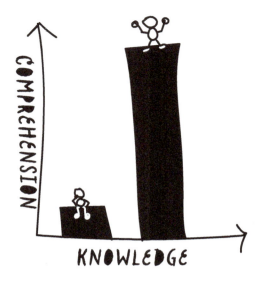

Take Charge: Conclusion and Reflective Questions

Background knowledge serves as a foundation for processing new information. This foundation allows readers to draw inferences, make connections to new concepts, and critically engage with texts. Background knowledge is more than just a collection of facts; it is a network of information that includes knowledge on a topic, prior experiences, and the connections between these pieces of information. In secondary classrooms, background knowledge becomes increasingly important for reading; texts and topics become increasingly more complex and more demanding of the learners' cognitive ability.

The glory of teaching is that we get to teach. We get to build students' knowledge and skills over the course of the year so they can be academically successful. Exposing students to new ideas and information and building their repository of stored information not only makes them better readers but also enhances their future learning.

- The more students know, the more they can learn. What background knowledge is most relevant to the concepts you're teaching, and have students already been exposed to it in previous grade levels or lessons?
- The less students know about a topic, the more challenging the reading becomes. What are some quick ways you can assess what students already know so you can determine your best entry point into a unit of study?
- Reading is a vehicle that helps students develop a deeper, more nuanced understanding of a topic. What background knowledge is necessary in your content for students to access challenging texts?
- How can you use multimodal texts to build background knowledge? How can you scaffold reading opportunities to build background knowledge before moving to grade-appropriate challenging texts?
- Identify an upcoming unit of instruction. Which background knowledge strategy will you use?

CHAPTER 3

Word Recognition
Free Up Cognitive Space, One Word at a Time

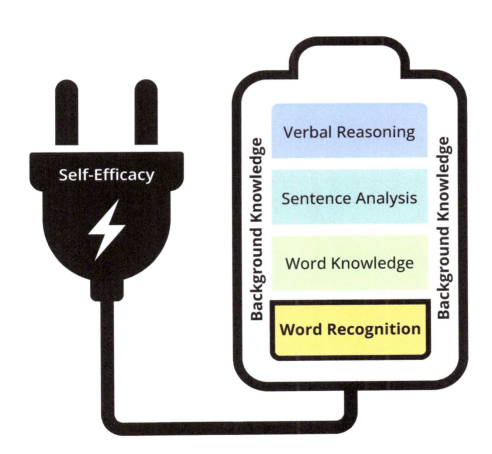

Many of us recall a familiar educational scenario from our own schooling: The teacher asked each student in class to read a paragraph aloud from a text. As the anticipation built, we counted the students ahead of us, mentally preparing to tackle the paragraph that would be assigned to us. With focused determination, we rehearsed that specific paragraph in our mind, striving to pronounce each word correctly so we sounded like we knew what we were doing. In that moment, our primary concern wasn't about listening to others or comprehending the text; it was simply about getting the words right.

However, sometimes things didn't go as planned. Perhaps a miscalculation in the rotation resulted in our assignment to a paragraph that was not the one we practiced! This triggered a wave of panic. Suddenly, the familiar words we rehearsed disappeared, replaced by unfamiliar ones.

As educators, we now know a host of reasons why this exercise is a thoroughly disproven approach to reading, whether it's called round-robin reading or popcorn reading or popsicle-stick reading. Ash and colleagues (2009) outlined three reasons drawn from their review of the research. The practice of round-robin reading

- interferes with the comprehension of the reader,
- reduces the comprehension of the other listeners, and
- provokes emotional distress in students reading below grade level and boredom among advanced readers.

In part, this interference with comprehension occurs because an outsized effort to recognize the words can crowd out the bandwidth needed to understand what is written. Unfortunately, even though no curriculum recommends it, many secondary teachers continue to pursue this approach (while expressing guilt), perhaps due to generational familiarity from their own schooling (Ash et al., 2009).

Reflecting on experiences like this, we have come to understand the profound impact of word recognition—the ability to decode a word quickly and effortlessly—on a student's confidence and academic success. These moments underscore the need to replace some traditional practices with evidence-based strategies for developing strong reading skills.

Word recognition serves as a foundational component at the base of the battery. This component underscores the fundamental ability to immediately recognize a word through a process of orthographic mapping, which we will discuss in further detail in the next section. Teachers can give students instruction on how to increase the words they know by sight by helping them understand how sounds connect to printed letters. In this chapter, we provide strategies for explicitly teaching multisyllabic words so students can focus on comprehending the content of the readings and course material.

Plug Into the Research

What happens when students do not recognize words they come across in their texts? Some students laboriously try to decode—to break apart the sounds—and in the process their comprehension suffers, hindering the connection between text information and background knowledge (National Institute of Child Health and Human Development, 2000). Some students, when silently reading, skip over words they don't immediately recognize, which also impedes their comprehension. While some might grasp a general sense of the meaning, skipping pronunciation makes them less likely to use that word in discussion, recall its definition, or spell the word correctly (Ehri, 2014). Either way, their **comprehension is stifled and they miss the opportunity to encounter more complex words.**

Therefore, it is not surprising that students with lower decoding abilities experience stagnant growth in reading comprehension (Wang, et al., 2019). Wang and colleagues tested a decoding threshold hypothesis by examining decoding and comprehension results among thirty-four thousand students in grades five through ten. Think of a threshold as the lower boundary of a skill. In this case, the skill is decoding. Wang and colleagues were able to determine that for older readers below the decoding threshold, reading comprehension gains were nil over multiple years, even though their teachers taught toward comprehension. "In other words, nothing seems to be effectively driving reading comprehension when decoding is insufficient" (p. 399).

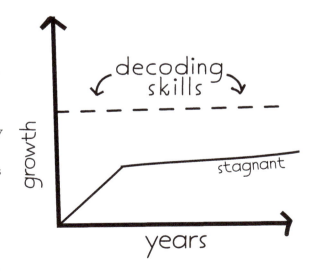

As noted earlier, older readers who fall below the decoding threshold need and deserve further intervention beyond what the classroom teacher is likely to be able to offer. Intervention approaches tailored for older readers are the subject of Chapter 7. This chapter focuses on students who are at or somewhat above the threshold but can benefit from additional instruction on reading strategies, and we share approaches you can incorporate into quality core instruction.

How Word Recognition Impacts Reading Comprehension

Many people mistakenly believe words are simply memorized and stored in our visual memory. The misconception is that when we read text, we simply retrieve the visual shapes of words from a mental Rolodex of words (Kilpatrick, 2016). It's akin to the idea that our brain just takes a picture of words and memorizes them. But that's not how it works.

The most current theory of word recognition centers on orthographic mapping, a process that enables readers to efficiently store and retrieve words from memory (Ehri, 2014; Kilpatrick, 2015). This ability has implications for students learning an additional language (Krepel et al., 2021). Orthographic mapping involves multiple processes: Readers must visually perceive letters, associate the letters with corresponding sounds, recognize word pronunciation, and connect pronunciation to meaning in their mind (see Figure 3.1). Like packaging goods for efficient transportation, orthographic mapping combines letters, pronunciation, and meaning into cohesive units. This packaging, or unitization, facilitates efficient word retrieval during reading.

Through orthographic mapping, students expand their sight-word vocabularies; sight words are those words they can read effortlessly and automatically. Sight words should not be confused with high-frequency words, which are those words that appear frequently in written language, such as *the*, *at*, and *were*. These high-frequency words are a subset of the reader's sight-word vocabulary and include those read frequently. Audiences of this book have words like *comprehension*, *vocabulary*, and *phonics* in their sight-word toolkit because they frequently encounter them. Although it may appear as memorization, readers quickly recall these terms because the sound-letter correspondences (more accurately described

CHAPTER 3 • Word Recognition

Figure 3.1 • How Orthographic Mapping Works

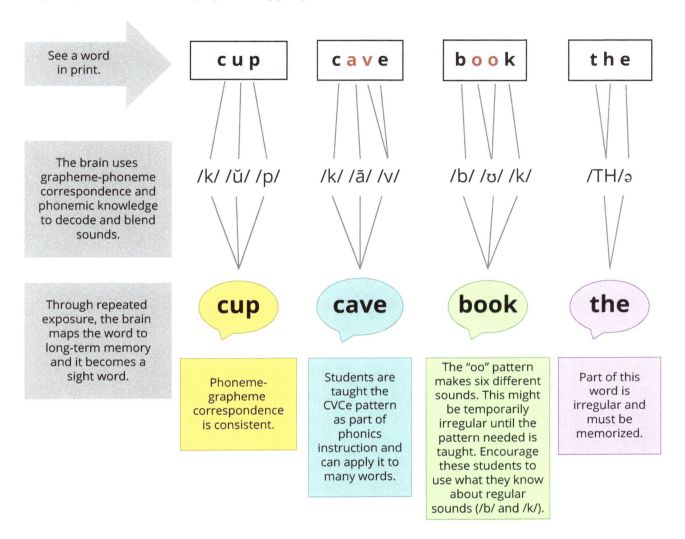

as grapheme-phoneme correspondences), the pronunciation of the word, and its connection to meaning have been packaged together.

Many of the words older readers encounter are multisyllabic, meaning they are comprised of two or more syllables. Skilled readers silently break apart multisyllabic words, especially unfamiliar ones, to figure out pronunciation and meaning. The place where two syllables meet is called the *syllable juncture,* and there are rules in English (and every alphabetic language) about how the syllables are determined. For example, we know *nakpin* and *semron* are probably nonwords because they violate the rules we have internalized about the place the syllables meet (Taft & Krebs-Lazendic, 2013). You certainly don't need to teach the particular rules, but it is important to help your students understand that syllables play a role in assisting a reader in the orthographic mapping and word recognition of a visually presented multisyllabic word.

Now consider how many general and discipline-specific multisyllabic words appear in your textbook and course materials. Your students encounter and must decode words like *overwhelming*, *refraction*, *binomial*, and *colonies* to read and understand texts. (In addition, readers deploy other skills, especially vocabulary and morphological awareness, which are the subject of the next chapter.) Breaking multisyllabic words into syllable chunks assists readers in mapping new words. As educators, understanding orthographic mapping and the role of syllables in word recognition helps us determine how to best support our students as they encounter new words across their classes each day.

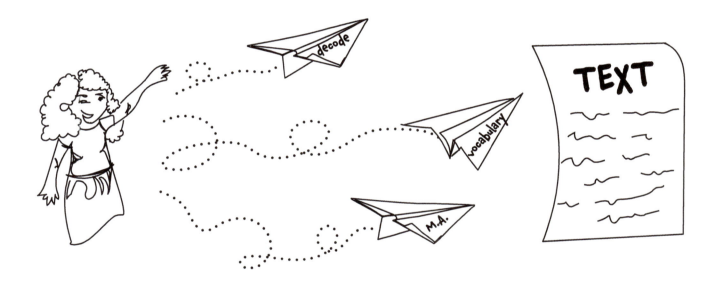

How Fluency Impacts Reading Comprehension

Word recognition plays a key role in another dimension of reading, which is fluency. Fluency is a reader's ability to decode a text accurately

and read orally or silently at a sufficient rate and expression to unlock meaning. Accurate decoding fuels fluency, and subsequently the reader's rate increases. Consequently, readers need less attention to unlock the sound of the words. As their accurate decoding and rate improve, their attention can more fully shift to comprehension, a phenomenon known as *automaticity* (LaBerge & Samuels, 1974). This is important because the brain's working memory— its ability to hold a finite number of units of meaning—is limited (Samuels & Decker, 2023). For example, think of your ability to remember an unfamiliar phone number only long enough to dial it. When readers recognize chunks of words rather than single letters, they can string these chunks together more smoothly.

Fluency practice is more common at the elementary level, yet research shows that fluency instruction and practice are needed for all students through high school (Paige et al., 2014), as it is linked to college readiness (Rasinski et al., 2017). More recently, fluency researchers have called for instruction at the middle and high school levels as a means to address what Kuhn and Schwanenflugel (2019) call "situational fluency... to help students develop both their comfort with whatever subject or genre they are responsible for reading and their metacognitive awareness, so when they experience discomfort with a text, they will have the capacity to deal with it" (p. 365).

The ability to read fluently requires pacing as well as accuracy. Read this text at the rate of one word per second:

Isolate. Each. Individual. Word. To. See. If. You. Are. Still. Able. To. Extract. The. Intended. Meaning. Of. An. Author. And. Read. With. Prosody. To. Determine. How. The. Concepts. Are. Linked. Together. Across. A. Text.

As you read, it's likely you had a more difficult time creating meaning of the text. Students who read less than sixty words per minute invariably struggle with comprehension because of the disfluent rate and connection between ideas. Skilled and experienced readers move their eyes in saccades (small steps): about four to five jerky movements every second. We all begin to do this naturally as we develop our word recognition skills, and this process contributes to our fluency. Skilled readers identify about ten to twelve letters per saccade, three or four to the left of their fixation and seven or eight to the right (Dehaene, 2009). Fluent readers are constantly moving their eyes ahead to the next words on a page to create meaning, and they are also cross-checking with saccades to recapture previously read words.

Reading fluency involves more than measures of rate and accuracy. *Prosody,* which is the ability to read silently or orally with expression that accurately reflects the text, is an important contributor to reading comprehension. Prosody is described as "[the] musical quality, [the] rhythm and flow, [which] makes reading sound effortless" and includes the ability to chunk phrases, shift intonation, and apply an appropriate pace and rhythm (Worthy & Broaddus, 2001/2002, p. 334). As one example, English teachers recognize the importance of prosodic oral reading in poetry and plays. A lack of prosody interferes significantly with understanding the nuances intended by the poet or playwright. But prosody is essential when reading any type of text, including informational and expository texts. Prosody is not only present in oral reading; it is also applied implicitly in silent independent reading. Take this sentence as an example:

After a minute but rapid examination of their weapons, the weary warriors ran down to the battlefield.

You may have stumbled momentarily on *minute*, correcting your silent pronunciation when you realized it was an adjective, not a noun. You paused at the comma, and you bundled together phrases such as *weary warriors* and *to the battlefield*. Each of these silent decisions aided you in comprehending the meaning of the sentence. To do so, you deployed several skills, including decoding, vocabulary, grammar, and syntax (the order of words), as well as background knowledge. Your ability to read silently—but with prosody— reflects your ability to understand the deeper meaning of what you read, whether it involves a character's emotions, a science writer's authoritative voice, or the directive tone of a series of steps in mathematics.

The Benefits of Repeated Reading and Choral Reading

There are two practices that serve as a throughline in the research on fluency instruction: repeated reading and choral reading. The first, repeated reading, draws on practice effects in learning, specifically in rehearsal and repetition. When students are engaged in repeated reading, they read the same piece of short text over a period of time, from a single class period to several days or even a week. In repeated reading, the goal is not to memorize the text but to read with increasing accuracy and sufficient pace and prosody. This technique is commonly recommended for students who need to strengthen their reading fluency, and teachers can easily integrate it into existing instruction, as these rehearsals are short (typically three to five minutes). Studies of repeated reading have demonstrated its effectiveness for students with reading difficulties and reading disabilities (Lee & Yoon, 2017).

The second practice incorporated in nearly all fluency instruction is choral reading. Unlike the round-robin reading discussed at the beginning of this chapter, choral reading requires previewing the text first, then reading in unison with the teacher. Because of the public performance element of choral reading, this practice is sometimes used when the reading contains quite a bit of dialogue, such as a play or a dialogue-intensive narrative passage, like Shakespeare's *Romeo and Juliet* (Hill, 2020). Choral reading can and should be a part of other content courses, too, not just English. For instance, history teachers can highlight powerful sentences contained in the Declaration of Independence with eighth-grade students. Similarly, science teachers can use choral reading to highlight the specific language in a physics textbook passage about Newton's third law of motion. Any written passage (even one composed by you) that is conceptually important to your instruction can do dual service as a choral reading passage.

Teacher Modeling for Word Recognition and Fluency

Teacher modeling has been widely recognized as an effective tool for building student proficiency and skill (Fisher & Frey, 2015; Methe & Hintze, 2003). The practice of teacher modeling serves as a direct demonstration. Teacher modeling has the added benefit of introducing target concepts, and it acquaints students with academic and topical language. Additionally, it helps students acquire the security and competence they need to be successful at the task when they try it independently. Modeling provides students with linguistic examples, which serve as the cognitive hooks on which they can hang new information. As learners become fluent

or familiar with these dimensions, they are cognitively free to refocus their attention on expanding and transferring the informational base to new situations.

Model word recognition and fluent reading using short pieces of text included in your lesson. For instance, you can select the first few sentences of a longer text your students will be reading and model how the reading should sound. Be sure learners are following along in their own copy of the text to strengthen the speech-to-print connection. This is especially effective when you have a text that begins with an interesting hook. (Be sure to rehearse a few times before reading it aloud so you can demonstrate the proper prosody needed.) Another modeling opportunity may exist in a paragraph containing some less familiar multisyllabic words. As you read, show learners how you broke the word down into its syllables. This approach provides students with the added benefit of hearing the word correctly pronounced, thus tying its usage to their silent reading.

Increase Your Battery Life

There is a lot to know about helping students develop automatic word recognition, but here are some important approaches to consider:

- **Model your thinking.** When reading or writing difficult words, model how to break apart the word. This helps students understand how to mimic the teacher's thought process.

- **Establish routines for introducing multisyllabic words for students to read the text more fluently and encourage students to apply these words in writing and discussions.** Initially, you may find that more complex or domain-specific words do not appear in your students' writing or conversation, which is often due to their lack of comfort with these words. Once you employ a routine to introduce this vocabulary, you can expect learners to use these words in their writing and discussions.

- **Include daily fluency practice.** As students increasingly automate their decoding, they become increasingly fluent readers. When students don't recognize words automatically, their ability to read fluently is compromised. To address this issue, you can employ targeted practices that use very little classroom time to aid your students in accessing grade-level texts and instruction.

- **Make thinking and reading audible and visible.** Allow students to read in small groups or partners so their reading fluency is audible. Unless teachers provide opportunities for learners to read aloud and express their knowledge and understanding of reading passages, it's hard to determine where the students' learning has broken down. Utilizing strategies like discussion and quick writes allows us to see how our students are processing information and making sense of texts, what gaps exist in their understanding, and what supports we need to put in place.

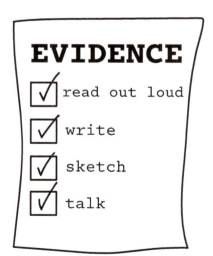

CHAPTER 3 • Word Recognition

Power Up Classroom Practice

For most educators reading this book, words in this passage can be considered sight words because you are reading through the sentences effortlessly. In secondary classrooms, there are specific words that teachers aim to introduce into the students' sight-word vocabulary. As we have noted, it's important for students to be able to recognize certain words automatically, both because they will repeatedly encounter these words in their studies of the content and because we want students to incorporate these words into their writing.

Importantly, learning to recognize words on sight is not limited to students in the elementary grades. Consider a word that is likely in your sight-word vocabulary: *Vygotsky*. When you read that word, you likely activate the pronunciation as well as the meaning: a Russian psychologist who gave us the zone of proximal development theory, sociocultural theory, and the term *inner speech*. However, your friends who are not educators would likely stumble on that word and have to try to figure it out, probably with very little understanding of the background knowledge the word activates.

There are many quick and efficient routines to develop students' sight-word vocabularies. After students experience direct instruction and oral practice, they should find these words have become ingrained, enabling their automatic word recognition, reducing their cognitive load, and allowing them to focus on comprehension of the content.

Classroom Practice: Word Recognition Strategies

There are several practices you can use in the classroom to help strengthen your students' ability to recognize words. More specifically, there are routines to build students' ability to recognize words at sight. Remember this requires that readers instantly connect the word's pronunciation, spelling, and meaning. Naturally, this takes practice and instruction.

Arm-Tapping Three-Minute Routine

The arm-tapping strategy is a short routine to introduce spelling, pronunciation, and reading of a word. For this exercise, teachers choose a word that is pivotal to an understanding students will need to achieve the

Video 3.1
Fire Science Arm Tapping
qrs.ly/s4fya4n

DIRECTIONS:
ARM-TAPPING

unit goals or day's learning intention. You can introduce the routine either prior to asking students to engage with the text or when noticing students are having difficulty with a word. Remember that if a student isn't accurately reading a word, it could impact their overall comprehension and decrease the likelihood they will use that word in their writing or discussion. Here is how to implement the routine:

1. Write the word on the screen, pronounce it aloud, and ask students to repeat the word.

2. Provide a student-friendly definition, use the word in a sentence, and offer other relevant information, such as the meaning of any word parts, related words, or a story about the history of the word.

3. Demonstrate how you break the word into syllable chunks by tapping your arm from your shoulder to your wrist. Students can participate by tapping the spelling of the word on their own arm while following your lead.

4. Ask students to say and write the word while looking at the word on the screen.

5. Ask students to say and write the word without referring to the screen.

6. Optional: Project a sentence from the day's reading that contains the word.

Let's look at an example of how this might work in practice. In a ninth-grade history class discussing vagrancy laws after the American Civil War, you might use the arm-tapping routine for the word *vagrancy* by following these steps.

1. Write *vagrancy* on the board and pronounce it: "vay-gruhn-see." Ask students to repeat the word.

2. Provide direct instruction: "The word *vagrancy* is the state of being a vagrant—a person who is said to either not have a place to live or a job to support themselves. Listen to this sentence: *Vagrancy laws criminalized men who were not working or not working at a job that was deemed as being sufficient.* As you read, you'll encounter words related to *vagrancy*, such as *vagrant* and *vagrancies*. There are a couple tricky things for us to notice when reading and spelling this word. Notice that even though there is an *a* in the second syllable, it makes more of a short *u* sound. Also notice that in the last syllable, the *c* makes the *s* sound. One more thing: Every syllable needs a vowel, so the *y* is the vowel and makes the long *e* sound. That's why it is pronounced 'vay-gruhn-see.'"

3. Demonstrate: "Watch me as I tap this word on my arm. I'll point to my shoulder and tap twice as you say the letters *v* and *a*. Then on the inside of the elbow I will tap four times as I simultaneously say the four letters *g-r-a-n*. Finally, I will say *c* and *y* as I tap my wrist twice. Then I'll say the word again. Now it's your turn to do it at the same time as me."

4. Write the word again, saying the letters in the same syllable chunks while arm tapping: v-a/ g-r-a-n/ c-y. Ask students to write the word while looking at the word on the screen.

5. Ask students to write *vagrancy* independently. Then continue with content learning.

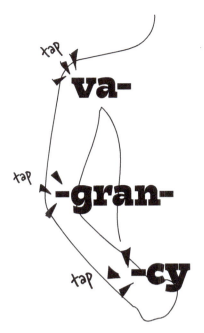

Flexible Word Chunking

Decoding multisyllabic words can be challenging, but using a flexible approach can support word recognition and pronunciation (Archer et al., 2003). Readers who practice flexible word chunking are willing to try different strategies for breaking the word up and for pronouncing word parts until they find what works best for a particular word.

Using the text your students will be reading in class, choose a multisyllabic word or two that learners might have a difficult time reading. Then ask students for ideas on how to break apart the word to read the word. Here are two specific ideas you can share with your students.

Segment Word Parts

Encourage students to first look through the whole word then look for recognizable parts within the word. Display the word separated into syllables to make reading it more manageable. Syllable instruction tends to work best for two- and three-syllable words; words that contain more than three syllables often contain affixes (collectively prefixes and suffixes) and therefore benefit more from instruction that includes morphological awareness (Bhattacharya, 2020), which we will further address in the next chapter. For example, let's say that as your eighth-grade social studies students are learning about the development of the U.S. Constitution, they encounter words such as *amendment* and *compromise*. You can display these words as shown in Figure 3.2 to assist students in pronouncing each syllable. It is important to note that pronunciation may vary depending on word form or context, so flexibility is key. Although there are patterns that you can teach explicitly, as students move up through the grade levels and words contain more syllables and parts, the consistency of the patterns is less reliable (Kerns, 2020).

Video 3.2
Flexible Word Chunking
qrs.ly/ybfya4q

Figure 3.2 • Segmenting Word Parts by Syllables

a-mend-ment

com-pro-mise

Adjust Vowel Sounds

Underline vowels or vowel teams in the word and demonstrate how readers can be flexible in the pronunciation of the vowel sound. For instance, if you were teaching a high school health class learning about disease patterns and how outbreaks of infectious diseases are investigated, you might identify the word *immune* as a word students might struggle to recognize and read automatically. To help them process the word, you could write it on the board, underline all the vowels, and then remind students they need to be flexible in the pronunciation of the vowel sounds. This approach helps students slow down and attend to each part of the word. It also gives you an opportunity to help them identify related words. For instance, if the reading contains variations (e.g., *immunology*), you could point them out to students and explain how those words are related to *immunity*.

As teachers, we also need to explicitly tell our students to use these decoding strategies when they encounter words. It is a mistake to assume that if we teach a strategy, students will use it. Often our students don't know they are supposed to generalize the strategies we have taught them when they are working to decode a word (Vaughn et al., 2000). We need to give learners numerous opportunities to practice chunking multisyllabic words and to use a mixture of these strategies to decode the word.

Classroom Practice: Building Fluency

Readers need to read fluently for comprehension, and regular practice is key to improvement. When learners repeat the same mentally demanding tasks over and over—in this case, reading—they become more fluent. Their ability to decode becomes automatic, but they need explicit instruction in how to break down words. The more fluent learners become with decoding, the more automatic they are with reading words—and the more room they have in their working memory to concentrate on meaning and what a text says.

Five-Day Fluency Routine

In a study of seventh- and eighth-grade students identified as struggling readers, Landreth and Young (2021) found that a ten-minute fluency routine they devised improved both student reading fluency and comprehension. Each day, teachers selected a short weekly reading of about 150 words and used it exclusively for this routine before moving forward with the content of the day's lesson. Think of this routine as a warm-up for the rest of the lesson.

CHAPTER 3 • Word Recognition

Figure 3.3 • Five-Day Fluency Routine

DAY	TEACHER ACTIONS	STUDENT ACTIONS	OPTIONS/TIPS
1	Present two texts and read aloud to students, modeling effective oral reading.	Listen as teacher models a reading of both texts; select a text to focus on for the week.	In time, teacher might also model poor reading and have students discuss; teacher might also record students reading on Day 1, then again on Day 5 and share with students to demonstrate growth.
2	Guide students in marking up script and dividing into parts, labeling parts as As and Bs; lead class in a word/text study; lead class in an echo/choral reading (teacher reads, class echoes).	Mark up script, divide into two parts, and label; participate in word/text study; participate in an echo/choral reading (all students read entire poem).	Reading chorally takes practice and may require several restarts. For secondary students there may be some apprehension at first. The teacher will also have to monitor to ensure that every student is participating.
3	Divide class into two groups; lead class in an antiphonal/choral reading group (group A reads part; group B reads part; teacher reads with both groups, leading the "chorus").	Participate in an antiphonal/choral reading, reading designated part, and follow along as the teacher leads.	Use teacher recorded read-alongs to practice.
4	Repeat antiphonal/choral reading, critique/discuss reading, then repeat reading.	Participate in antiphonal/choral reading; listen to and apply comments from critique in second reading.	Have students switch parts; have students read with a partner or a group of four; at some point, the teacher should gradually release responsibility of the critique over to students.
5	Lead the class in a final reading; prepare a concluding activity (mini-performance, self-evaluation, etc.).	Participate in final reading and concluding activity.	On Day 5, the selection will be added to the students' practice folders. At the end of each six weeks, the class will prepare a performance created from the practiced texts.

Source: Used with permission of Taylor & Francis Informa UK Ltd - Journals, from *Developing fluency and comprehension with the secondary fluency routine*, Landreth, S. J., & Young, C., vol 114, 2021; permission conveyed through Copyright Clearance Center, Inc.

As you examine this approach in Figure 3.3, you'll find there are several conditions in the five-day routine that mirror research-based fluency instruction, including teacher modeling, repeated readings, and choral readings of familiar text.

Classroom Practice: Read This to Me

By the time students get to middle school, reading is largely silent and independent. Consequently, we don't always hear when our students decode incorrectly or read disfluently, and thus we cannot provide them with appropriate support. Read This to Me is a strategy that teachers can use

Video 3.3
Read This
qrs.ly/z5fya4t

routinely throughout the week to facilitate student reading and provide targeted feedback to support accurate word recognition and fluency. These brief yet impactful sessions typically last around two minutes and provide students with the feedback they need not only to read but also to comprehend how to solve problems. The following steps outline this simple yet impactful strategy:

1. During independent or collaborative tasks, select a section of text that your students have been working on and quietly ask a student to read a portion of the text aloud so only you can hear it.

2. Listen attentively and offer feedback on word accuracy and fluency.

3. After providing feedback, ask the student to reread the same passage to ensure that your feedback was understood (because the learner implemented it effectively).

Repeat this practice daily with different students to ensure feedback for all students.

As an example, Daniel Falomo, an Integrated Math 3 teacher, had his students studying statistical tools and tasked them with applying what he had taught them by solving some problems independently. One problem involved a statistical analysis on the effectiveness of a new antibiotic. During independent practice, Mr. Falomo approached a student and requested that they quietly read the problem aloud to him. He found he needed to correct the student's pronunciation of *petri dish* and checked to make sure the student knew about this piece of lab equipment. He also modeled the proper phrasing of a complex sentence that contained multiple clauses, as the student's inflection suggested they weren't fully comprehending it. As a final step, Mr. Falomo then asked the student to reread the word problem aloud and asked a few questions to confirm the student understood the information in the word problem.

Classroom Practice: Whole Class Choral Reading

Whole class choral reading involves students reading aloud simultaneously with the teacher. Think of choral reading like a synchronized chorus performance. While the teacher leads the reading, all students contribute their voices to match the teacher's. It's usually best to repeat this practice regularly, either using the same text for a couple of days or different texts centered around a common theme or topic. The strategy typically requires about three to five minutes of the class period. As noted earlier, many teachers opt to incorporate this exercise at the beginning of the class period because the structured routine helps create a classroom energy that primes students for the work ahead during the class period. Here's how it works:

Video 3.4
Choral Reading
qrs.ly/4vfya4w

Preparing for Choral Reading

- Select a text that is rich in content and supports the learning of the unit of study.
- Ensure that each student has access to the text, whether through a shared electronic document or hard copy.

During Choral Reading

- Provide a brief introduction to the passage and ensure that all students have their eyes on the text.
- Model a fluent reading of the entire passage on the first day while students read along silently.
- On subsequent days, engage students in chorally reading the passage. It is helpful to use a countdown so all students begin reading at the same time.
- Listen for reading miscues and model the corrections as needed.
- Repeat this passage every day for the week.

After Choral Reading

- Choose from a variety of postreading activities to reinforce the idea that the purpose of reading fluently and with expression is that it helps with comprehension.
- Have students generate questions based on the passage and discuss answers.
- Ask students to summarize the selection that was read.
- Guide students to identify five keywords and use them to create a summary sentence.
- Prompt students to create a visual sketch that represents the reading.

Teachers in all subject areas can use this strategy to simultaneously support reading and the development of content knowledge.

Voices From the Field

Math teachers often use choral reading of a math problem before analyzing the quantities and the questions being asked. In a seventh-grade math class, Liam Baker used this fluency routine to support math concepts and vocabulary. For example, on Monday Mr. Baker introduced the text "What is a variable?" He read it aloud to the class, modeling his fluent reading. The students continued to interact with the text each day according to the routine, which variously included repeated readings and choral readings. Reflecting on the benefits of this approach, Mr. Baker noted, "This is how we start off each period, and I really love how instructional minutes are

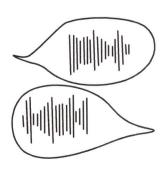

maximized. Also, I find it helpful to make sure some key terms are solidified, and students have multiple opportunities to read and say those key terms to support their math understanding."

Ana Loaiza, a tenth-grade English teacher, uses the fluency routine outlined in Table 3.1. As part of an upcoming unit, her students were going to read an excerpt from the novel *Monster* by Walter Dean Myers and an excerpt from *To Kill a Mockingbird* by Harper Lee. Ms. Loaiza wanted to provide some background knowledge for this unit, so in the previous week, the students read some informational texts about the American justice system. She used the fluency routine to support word recognition and fluency while building vital background knowledge. Ms. Loaiza explained,

> There are so many benefits to this strategy. My favorite thing is how much my students appreciate the routine. It's fast-paced, but they know what to expect. And the questions they develop on Thursday have really started to impress me. Also, when I walk around as students whisper-read, I can provide some quick individual feedback. But sometimes there

Table 3.1 • Ten-Minute Daily Fluency Routine to Support Content Knowledge and Vocabulary

MONDAY	TUESDAY	WEDNESDAY	THURSDAY	FRIDAY
Teacher models the text selection. (two min.)	Teacher uses the choral reading strategy on a selection of the text. (two min.)	Teacher uses the choral reading strategy on a selection of the text. (two min.)	Partner A reads to Partner B. Partner B gives feedback based on accuracy of words and expression. (three min.)	Students read the same section of the text in a whisper voice as the teacher walks around to listen. (three min.)
Students read the same section of the text in a whisper voice as the teacher walks around to listen. (three min.)	Students read the same section of the text in a whisper voice as the teacher walks around to listen. (three min.)	Students read the same section of the text in a whisper voice as the teacher walks around to listen. (three min.)	Partner B reads to Partner A. Partner A gives feedback based on accuracy of words and expression. (three min.)	Students develop questions based on the text. (two min.)
Students engage in a partner share: "What is this text mainly about?" (three min.)	Teacher poses a text-dependent question and partners discuss. (three min.)	Teacher asks a question that requires inferential thinking. Partners discuss. (three min.)	Writing: Students respond to text-dependent questions. (four min.)	Writing: Students choose one of the questions that were developed and independently craft a written response. (five min.)
Students are chosen at random (after the partner share opportunity) to summarize the main point of the text. (two min.)	Students are chosen at random (after the partner share opportunity) to respond to the question. (two min.)	Students are chosen at random (after the partner share opportunity) to respond to the question. (two min.)		

will be a sentence that I hear several students struggle with, so I might use one or two minutes of our fluency routine to do a deeper dive into that sentence. It might be a word they are struggling to decode, or it could be the structure of the sentence, but we analyze the sentence to ensure we are getting meaning from the words. That helps with their fluency, and in turn with the comprehension of the text as a whole.

Take Charge: Conclusion and Reflective Questions

Enhancing students' word recognition skills is a vital component to building confident, skilled readers who can access the content of classrooms through reading. Students achieve word recognition through the process of orthographic mapping. The research on orthographic mapping helps us as educators understand that we need to provide students with explicit instruction on how the sounds of a word are connected to strings of letters, and how the pronunciation of the word is connected to the concepts represented by that word. This web of connections between the sound, spelling, and meaning of words offers students the opportunity to store this information in a way that is easier to retrieve from memory. Older readers encounter an increasing number of multisyllabic words that can cause them to stumble in their reading. We can use strategies like arm-tapping routines and flexible word chunking to demonstrate the application of word recognition strategies for multisyllabic words to move terms into students' growing sight-word bank.

Word recognition is an important contributor to reading fluency, which includes the rate, accuracy, and expression used when reading. Teachers can support reading fluency by using strategies such as listening to students read and implementing routine choral reading practices. This chapter underscores the critical importance of word recognition and fluency in laying the groundwork for reading comprehension. Think about how you might take charge of your students' word recognition and fluency abilities.

- The ability to read accurately and fluently goes hand in hand with reading comprehension, but so much of secondary reading is silent. How can you build in opportunities to hear students read aloud to determine if inaccurate word recognition or disfluent reading is impacting their comprehension?
- Students who struggle with word recognition and reading fluency often do not want to read aloud to the whole class, lest they risk

embarrassment. How can you use small group or whole class choral reading to ease anxiety while ensuring they get the exposure and practice of discipline-specific reading? How might you help students build sight-word automaticity with academic words to increase their reading fluency?

- Effort control is important for self-regulation, and reading disfluency can create frustration. How might you encourage students' efforts to engage in reading without lowering the expectations of content?

- Developing schema automation for reading is critical so decoding becomes effortless and automatic. How might you use repeated and choral reading to support students in building automaticity and becoming more fluent readers?

CHAPTER 4

Word Knowledge
The More You Know, the More You Can Learn

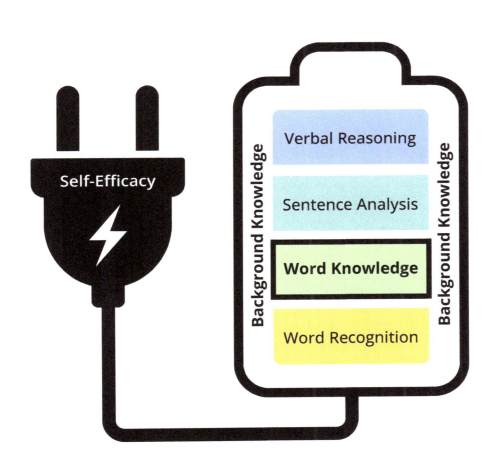

Consider the following paragraph:

> A ˈkrɪtɪkᵊl, ˌɪndɪˈpɛndənt and ɪnˈvɛstɪɡeɪtɪvprɛs is the ˈlaɪfblʌd of ˈany dɪˈmɒkrəsi. The prɛs must be free from steɪt ˌɪntəˈfɪərᵊns. It must have the ˌiːkəˈnɒmɪkstrɛŋθ to stand up to the ˈblændɪʃmənts of ˈɡʌvᵊnməntəˈfɪʃᵊlz. It must have səˈfɪʃᵊnt ˌɪndɪˈpɛndəns from ˈvɛstɪd ˈɪntrɛsts to be bəʊld and ɪnˈkwaɪərɪŋ without fɪər or ˈfeɪvə. It must ˈdʒɔɪ the prəˈtɛkʃᵊn of the ˌkɒnstɪˈtjuːʃᵊn, so it can prəˈtɛkt ˈour raɪts as ˈsɪtɪzᵊnz. (Mænˈdɛlə, 1994)

What is the main idea of this paragraph? What is the speaker's claim? How does he feel about the role of the press? Chances are good that if you're fluent in the International Phonetic Alphabet, you could answer these questions easily. If not, maybe you were able to pick up on "independent and investigative press." Perhaps you began drawing on your background knowledge to start guessing other words related to the press, but even so, for you the meaning might still have been cloudy. Similarly, when students lack the ability to read multisyllabic words or don't understand what words mean, their comprehension suffers. In this chapter, we emphasize that for students to gain depth and breadth of word knowledge, learning must be combined with other language components (listening, speaking, writing) and content knowledge to promote significant impact on student reading comprehension.

Plug Into the Research

Word knowledge encompasses an understanding of a word's meaning, its pronunciation, and its various uses within different contexts. It also involves recognizing a word's morphological structure, such as its root forms and affixes, and its connections to other words in terms of synonyms, antonyms, and semantic fields. Word knowledge requires that students both recognize words in text and comprehend their meanings to make sense of the text. Word knowledge is an essential bridge between decoding and reading comprehension (Perfetti & Stafura, 2014).

While word knowledge in isolation is not a guarantee of reading comprehension (for instance, you can know a list of vocabulary words but not be able to understand a text passage using the same words), word knowledge represents a student's ability to further consolidate the three classes of knowledge sources used in reading (Perfetti & Stafura, 2014, p. 24):

CHAPTER 4 • Word Knowledge

- Linguistic knowledge (knowledge of how the language works)
- Orthographic knowledge (decoding knowledge)
- General knowledge (knowledge about the world, including knowledge of text forms, such as text genres)

Video 4.1
Word Knowledge
qrs.ly/2pfya51

Word knowledge, also known more commonly as *vocabulary knowledge* grows over a lifetime of experiences. For people of all ages, not only does our vocabulary grow in terms of the number of words and word phrases we know but it also deepens. We continually refine and expand on our knowledge of the meanings, context, and nuances of words in relationship to one another. For this reason, vocabulary knowledge is an unconstrained skill, meaning it expands across our entire adult lives (Paris, 2005).

Although there is no one best way to teach or assess vocabulary development for every student, ample evidence supports the notion that word meanings are learned in multiple ways (Nagy et al., 1987). These range from incidentally learning words while reading or listening to texts and conversations to explicit teacher-led instruction of words (Hall et al., 2017; Uchihara et al., 2019). There also are some ineffective ways to teach vocabulary, such as the "assign-define-test" approach that has been common in many secondary classrooms.

Two fundamental pieces of word knowledge that contribute to comprehension are breadth and depth. *Breadth* refers to how many words and word phrases someone knows, while *depth* refers to how well they know terms and related words. Beck and her colleagues (2013) make an important distinction between shallow and deeper word knowledge. When it comes to word knowledge, a student with shallow knowledge might know a basic definition and a limited application of the term. Deeper word knowledge comes with knowing multiple meanings of the word (when applicable), understanding its relationship to other terms, perceiving a strong link to the concepts it represents, and having the ability to position it within a larger schema. Importantly, shallow and deep knowledge are not opposites. Rather, shallow knowledge precedes deeper knowledge. With deeper knowledge, our students' ability to use a word or word phrase in different contexts, as well as in writing and speaking, grows. As Nagy and Scott (2000) stated, "Knowing a word means being able to do things with it" (p. 237).

Word learning also includes knowing how words work. Students need to understand morphological elements, including prefixes, suffixes, root words, base words, and word families. This knowledge gives them access to understanding more words. Nagy and Anderson (1984) estimated that about 60 percent of the words learners encounter in middle

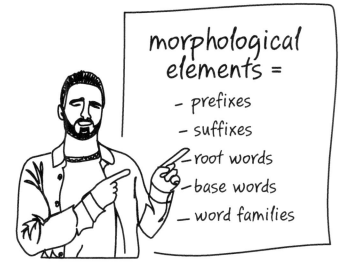

and high school contain complex morphemes (the smallest units of meaning) that are transparent enough in structure for students to accurately infer word meaning (e.g., *neurogenesis, dictatorship, algebraic*). Thus, learning words and word parts is helpful for boosting vocabulary.

Unsurprisingly, there's a strong relationship between the number of words known by a reader and the reader's degree of comprehension. In fact, vocabulary is among the strongest predictors of reading comprehension, particularly for middle and high school students (Ahmed et al., 2016). Further, vocabulary is a variable that differentiates struggling comprehenders from adequate comprehenders (Oslund et al., 2018). To help bridge the gap, teachers must incorporate systematic opportunities for direct teaching of necessary vocabulary and provide multiple opportunities for students to encounter new words in complex texts.

Multisyllabic words are comprised of multiple morphemes, each of which carries meaning. For readers, knowledge of the morphology of the word can unlock the meaning of new terms. For example, you might be unfamiliar with the term *astrometeorology*, but your knowledge of morphemes can give you a good running start. *Astro-* refers to stars, and *meteor* has something to do with the atmosphere. Now add the suffix *-ology*, which you know means the study of something. While you may not be all the way to its definition (the study of the star's effect on weather), you have a toehold. With that in mind, it takes deeper knowledge to know that astrometeorology is a pseudoscience because astrology is not a legitimate predictor of weather. (By the way, the word part *pseudo-* in *pseudoscience* signals that it is a fake science.)

How Students Learn New Words and Word Phrases

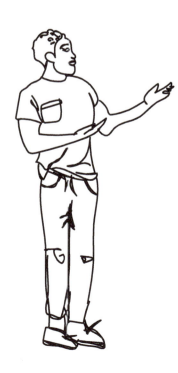

Students learn vocabulary in two ways: *direct word learning*, which involves a teacher explicitly teaching or explaining words and concepts; and *indirect word learning*, where students are exposed to words through listening and reading. **Multiple exposures to vocabulary are necessary**, in part because word knowledge is incremental and evolves with repeated use (Frishkoff et al., 2011). Leading vocabulary researchers such as Elleman and colleagues (2009) and Ogle and colleagues (2015) have noted that there are several components of comprehensive vocabulary instruction for adolescents:

- Teacher-directed explicit instruction of words and morphology in student-friendly descriptions, explanations, and examples
- Multiple exposures to vocabulary in rich content-based contexts, including students constructing images and deepening knowledge of words and related words through writing
- Active student engagement in using, listening for, writing, paraphrasing, redefining, and discussing new words

Based on the number of words students need to gain over the course of their K–12 experience, it's impossible for educators to directly teach all the words learners will encounter. While educators should be strategic about the discipline-specific words they teach explicitly, fostering our students' independent word learning is also crucial for helping them in our classrooms (Ellman et al., 2019). We can accomplish this by exposing our students to rich academic texts, fostering word consciousness, and teaching them word-attack strategies through context, word parts, and morphology (Ogle et al., 2015).

The Role of Morphological Awareness in Word Knowledge

Multisyllabic words permeate the materials adolescents read, and the number of terms they encounter explodes in middle and high school (Nagy & Anderson, 1984). Nagy and Anderson estimated that by ninth grade, students need to know 88,500 word families, which are words related in meaning but altered by affixes. For example, the word *significant* is part of a word family that includes *significance, significantly, insignificance, insignificantly,* and *signified*. This word family contains prefixes (*in-* in *insignificance*) and suffixes (*-ly* in *significantly*). Prefixes are quite useful in understanding multisyllabic words. Table 4.1 contains a list of the most common prefixes.

Video 4.2
Morphology
qrs.ly/nufya54

Prefixes and suffixes are morphemes; they carry a meaning that shapes the definition of the root or base they are modifying. Morphemes fall into two categories (see Table 4.2):

- A free morpheme can stand on its own as its own word. The compound word *afterthought* consists of two free morphemes: *after* and *thought*.
- A bound morpheme cannot stand on its own as a word, such as *-ful* in *thoughtful*. These are the prefixes and suffixes that modify the meaning of the word and the part of speech.

By middle school, an estimated 60 to 80 percent of academic vocabulary is morphologically complex (Brown, 1947; Nagy & Anderson, 1984). Further, morphological instruction within the context of vocabulary instruction is regarded as especially effective for secondary students. A well-regarded large-scale study of multilingual and monolingual middle school learners found that vocabulary instruction that included meanings of taught words, their morphological components, and their use in informational texts

Table 4.1 • High-Utility Prefixes

PREFIX	COMMON MEANING	EXAMPLES
un-	not	unhappy
	opposite of, contrary to	unrest
re-	again, anew	rebuild
	backward, back	replay
in-, im-, -ir-, il-	not	inactive, immobile, irrational, illegal
dis-	not	dissimilar
	opposite of	disfavor
	remove	discount
en-, em-	put or go into or onto	encage, embed
	to cause to be	endear, emblaze
non-	not	nonhuman
in-, im-	into, inside, within	inbound, immerge, implode
over-	above, too much	overuse
mis-	bad, wrong	misconduct
	failure, lack	misfire
sub-	below, under	subsoil
	secondary	subplot
	less than complete	subhuman
pre-	before, in front of	prehistoric
inter-	between, among	international
fore-	before, in front of	forerunner
de-	make opposite of	decriminalize
	remove	dethrone
	reduce	declass
trans-	across, beyond	transatlantic
	change	transcribe
	through	transfer
super-	above, over	superimpose
	superior	superfine
	excessive	supercharge
semi-	half	semicircle
	partial	semiconscious
	happening two times	semimonthly
anti-	opposite	antigravity
	counteracting	antibody
mid-	middle	midstream
under-	beneath, below, less in degree	underage

Source: Adapted from the works of White and colleagues (1989) as well as Sedita (2009).

CHAPTER 4 • Word Knowledge

Table 4.2 • Example of Free and Bound Morphemes in a Word

BIODEGRADABLE		
MORPHEME	**MORPHEME TYPE**	**MORPHEME MEANING**
Grade [hard]	Free morpheme	A level, rank, or quality
Bio- [life]	Bound morpheme	Prefix that refers to a living state of being
-able	Bound morpheme	Suffix that means capable of being

advanced learning for both groups in as little as eighteen weeks (Lesaux et al., 2010). Another compelling reason for you to include morphological instruction in your classroom is its association with older students' ability to spell with accuracy (Templeton, 1983).

Morphological awareness extends beyond affixes and includes knowledge of Latin and Greek root words. These comprise many of the subject-area vocabulary of secondary courses: Examples include *oligarthy* in history, *antagonist* in English, *carcinogenic* in biology, *kinesiology* in physical education, *aquamarine* in art, and *circumference* in math. The English language is influenced by Latin and Greek, as are other Indo-European languages, such as Spanish and French. Therefore, cognates, which are words that have a similar construction and meaning, are useful for multilingual learners whose first language is similarly influenced (e.g., *circumference* and *circunferenica*).

The morphology of affixes, along with Latin and Greek roots, form a strong pair that is predictive of a significant portion of the English language (Henry, 2017). Brown (1947) stated that the twelve Latin roots and two Greek roots listed in Table 4.3, when combined with the common prefixes, formed one hundred thousand words. Understandably, he referred to these roots as "master words."

Table 4.3 • Brown's Master Words

ROOT	MEANING	ORIGIN	EXAMPLE
tent, ten, tin, tain	to have, hold	Latin	detain
mit, miss, mitt	to send	Latin	intermittent
cap, capt, cip, cept	to take, seize	Latin	precept
fer	to bear, carry	Latin	offer
sta, stat, sist	to stand	Latin	insist
graph, gram	to write	Greek	monograph
log, ology	science	Greek	epilogue
spect	to look, see	Latin	aspect
plic, plex, ply	to fold, bend	Latin	uncomplicated
tens, tend, tent	to stretch	Latin	nonextended
duc, duct	to lead, make	Latin	reproduction
pos, pon	to put, place	Latin	indisposed
fac, fic, fact	to make, do	Latin	oversufficient
scribe, script	to write	Latin	mistranscribe

We're used quite a bit of vocabulary in this section. We hope Table 4.4 serves as a quick review of terms associated with morphology.

Table 4.4 • Morphology Terms

COMPONENT	DEFINITION	EXAMPLE
Prefix	An affix added to the beginning of a word to create a new meaning	*mis-*, meaning wrongly or not, as in *misunderstand*
Suffix	An affix added to the end of a root or base word to create a new meaning	*-ive*, meaning having the quality of, as in *divisive*
Root or base	A morpheme or morphemes to which affixes or other bases may be added	*cycle-* meaning an interval of time, as in *cyclical* (note the suffix *-al*)
Cognate	Two words having the same ancestral language and meaning	*Tragedy* and the Spanish word *tragedia* both mean an event that causes great suffering.
Derivational word families	A group of words that are related because of their root or base	*ambiguous, ambiguity, unambiguous* *brief, briefly, brevity* *energy, energetic, energies*

We recognize the challenge that remains when you are considering which words to teach. In the next section, we address the topic of word selection.

But Which Words?

Selecting words for instruction is among the most controversial topics in vocabulary instruction. There simply is not a single comprehensive list that teachers can use to teach the words students need to know. However, there are several useful lists that target an essential dimension, such as the Background Knowledge Word List (Marzano & Pickering, 2005) and the Academic Word List (Coxhead, 2000). But even when you are armed with those lists, you'll likely find that your students and classes will differ in terms of the words that you need to teach.

There are several different determinants to help teachers select vocabulary words worthy of being taught. We favor a list of questions teachers can use to determine which words should be the focus of explicit instruction (Fisher & Frey, 2023). This list draws from the work of Michael Graves, William Nagy, and others.

CHAPTER 4 • Word Knowledge

- Representative
  - Is the word representative of a family of words that students should know?
  - Is the concept represented by the word critical to understanding the text?
  - Is the word a label for an idea that students need to know?
  - Does the word represent an idea that is essential for understanding another concept?
- Repeated useage
  - Will the word be used again in this text? If so, does the word occur often enough to be redundant?
  - Will the word be used again during the school year?
- Transportable
  - Will the word be used in group discussions?
  - Will the word be used in writing tasks?
  - Will the word be used in other content or subject areas?
- Can be analyzed contextually
  - Can students use context clues to determine the correct or intended meaning of the word without instruction? If so, the word may not be worthy of instruction.
- Can be analyzed structurally
  - Can students use structural analysis to determine the correct or intended meaning of the word without instruction? If so, the word may not be worthy of instruction.
- Cognitive load
  - Have I identified too many words for students to successfully integrate?

Carefully considering each of these questions will help you select words worthy of instructional attention.

 **Increase Your Battery Life**

There is a lot to know about developing word knowledge, but here are some important approaches to consider:

- **Maximizing instructional time involves ending harmful and ineffective practices as much as it involves inputting new practices.** Avoid the following:

o *Giving students word lists to memorize for a weekly test.* When students memorize word lists, they tend to regurgitate them for a test and forget them immediately after. Students need to see how word parts can be used to form other words. They need to see the connections and transferability of word parts and how to use them in conjunction with other morphemes to make sense of morphologically complex words (like *consolable*, or *augmentative*, or the relationship between *mitochondria* and *mitochondrion*).

o *Front-loading too many vocabulary words.* When too many words are taught ahead of the unit, it overtaxes learners' working memory. The result is that students do not learn the words and thus do not transfer them into the context of reading.

o *Having students copy words and definitions, believing the copying will result in encoding.* Copying words and definitions in and of itself does not result in the transfer to long-term memory. Effective vocabulary teaching requires us to go beyond just the dictionary definitions; context matters to help students build appropriate knowledge.

- **It's impossible to teach all the words students will encounter in a text.** Foster word consciousness, which is an awareness of words, through intentional teaching. Word consciousness helps students see their own gaps. Exposing students to complex texts is important for students to develop depth and breadth of vocabulary.

- **Students need multiple opportunities to engage with vocabulary and morphological parts before this information becomes stored into their long-term memory.** There are dozens of different strategies you may wish to use to teach vocabulary, and we will outline several of them later in this chapter. Regardless of the strategies you choose, you should implement routines for vocabulary learning and give students multiple opportunities to authentically and meaningfully interact with new words.

- **Teach related words so students understand the connections between words.** For example, in a world history class, a teacher can introduce the word *fascism* and then write the related word *fascist* to help students automatically read both those words in the text and understand the differences in spelling and meaning.

- **Create routines for word learning.** Students need opportunities for speaking and writing (expressive language) to generate the greatest retention. The more ways a student can see, hear, and use a word, the more likely it will stick. Use images, tables, diagrams, examples, nonexamples, and analogies to give students an increasing understanding of the vocabulary so they can create stronger mental representations of what words mean.

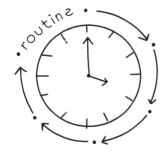

Power Up Classroom Practice

Let's apply research on word knowledge to instructional practices that support students' access to content. Here are the classroom practices we will explore:

- Fostering word consciousness
  - Word journals
  - Self-assessment
- Teaching individual words, morphology, and word parts
  - Direct teach
- Providing rich and varied learning experiences
  - Routines for building academic language
  - Hexagonal thinking
  - Affinity mapping
  - Word walls
- Teaching word-learning strategies

Classroom Practice: Fostering Word Consciousness

As educators, we want our students to develop *word consciousness*, or the ability to recognize when they don't know a word or when they lack a deep understanding of the meaning of the word. Readers with word consciousness often show a genuine interest in words and actively seek out opportunities to acquire new words to expand their vocabularies. They enjoy exploring new words, learning their meanings, and discovering how words can be used effectively in different contexts.

Word Journals

Although research does not support asking students to look up words and copy the definitions, teachers can have students choose their own vocabulary to create a self-selected glossary that fosters word consciousness and gives them ownership of the text. Shanahan (2019), a former president of the International Literacy Association, argues, "When readers get used to noticing their lack of knowledge of particular words, they will be more likely to try to resolve those gaps when reading." Word journals give students the opportunity to choose unfamiliar words

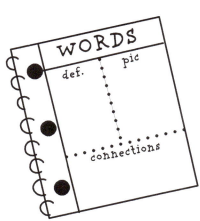

and also, by teaching others, contribute to their peers' understanding of new words. Here's how the process of using word journals works:

1. Students skim a chapter or text to identify unfamiliar words and words they think will be important to understanding the reading.

2. In their word journal, students paraphrase or summarize definitions and draw pictures to help consolidate their understanding.

3. As the learning progresses, students revisit their words and definitions to update them, explain them, revise them, and build connections.

The role of updating in this approach is crucial. Students need multiple opportunities to interact with new vocabulary words and update their mental lexicon of words based on new learning. To consolidate their understanding, students can utilize generative strategies like concept mapping, sketching, or teaching others to connect words and deepen their existing understanding.

Self-Assessment

Beck and McKeown (1991) note there are levels or stages of vocabulary learning: unknown, acquainted, and established. Teaching students to pay attention to words fosters word consciousness. It allows them to notice when they know or don't know a term well, whether they are familiar or unfamiliar with a word, and the level of understanding they possess about a word or group of words. Teachers can use the following scale for pre- and postassessment:

Video 4.3
Self-Assessment
qrs.ly/mrfya57

- **0:** I don't know this word.
- **1:** I've seen this word, and I can read/pronounce it.
- **2:** I can define this word and use it in a sentence.
- **3:** I can explain this word and its meaning(s).
- **4:** I can connect this word to other words.

You can also identify common themes based on your students' preassessments to determine the words you need to explicitly teach them. You can gather this information in a digital form, such as Google Forms, for ease of data collection. Not only can you individualize this information for each class but you can also note trends and patterns across classes to determine the words for explicit instruction.

Classroom Practice: Teaching Individual Words, Morphology, and Word Parts

Video 4.4
Self-Assessment
Interview
qrs.ly/5xfya59

Vocabulary knowledge is critical, and the number of words students know impacts the rate at which they learn future words. For students to be successful, we need to incorporate an intentional vocabulary-teaching approach as part of the overall classroom experience, rather than as a series of random activities designed to episodically engage our students in word learning. For some words, students need us to provide direct explanations of what it means, what it is, what it isn't, and representations of what it looks like.

Direct Instruction

We can't directly teach every word students need to know, so it's important to choose words and morphological elements that are critical to the discipline. Here are a few suggestions on how to maximize your explicit instruction of individual words or morphological elements:

- **Explain the word in student-friendly terms, linking to students' prior knowledge.** Dictionary definitions are not always the most beneficial route because students cannot form a mental representation of what the word is or means.

- **Provide examples and nonexamples when appropriate.** Knowing what something isn't is often as helpful as knowing what it is.

- **Use visuals to bridge the learning.** Bridge the word with graphic or multimedia representations.

- **Compare and contrast concepts through analogies.** Comparisons help students link prior knowledge to new learning so they develop both depth and breadth of vocabulary. By connecting new material to prior knowledge, students create stronger connections and pathways in their brains for organizing and retrieving target vocabulary. Provide examples that draw on familiar analogies. For example, an explanation of the word *sequence* might include an analogy to a staircase.

- **Have students pronounce the words with you.** Pronouncing the new words correctly gives students more touchpoints with the concepts by increasing their expressive language. They hear the word, see the word, and say the word to connect the spelling to pronunciation.

Classroom Practice: Providing Rich and Varied Learning Experiences

Word learning doesn't exist in a vacuum or in an isolated lesson within a unit. Teachers need to provide students with multiple exposures to hear, see, read, write, and discuss word meanings in the context of sentences and paragraphs so they can develop an increasing depth of understanding. Much of this chapter has been devoted to vocabulary learning, which is gaining knowledge of words and phrases. But vocabulary terms do not exist in isolation. They are components of fully formed thoughts and ideas, spoken and written. If vocabulary forms the bricks of a sentence, academic language is the mortar.

Video 4.5
Routines for
Academic Language
Concept Sort
qrs.ly/wyfya5f

Much like building a strong structure, vocabulary should be accompanied by academic language-building opportunities.

Routines for Building Academic Language

Copying definitions to learn words is less effective than more interactive approaches, such as students sketching or mapping words, discussing terms, and generating connections (Wright & Cervetti, 2017). One solid way for students to learn vocabulary is to couple it with academic language. To consolidate their word knowledge, students must use the target vocabulary in their interactions with others as well as in their writing. When we give learners multiple opportunities to apply new words, their likelihood of encoding the words into their long-term memory increases.

Discussion and interaction are effective for vocabulary development because they allow students to use their newly acquired vocabulary along with academic language. In addition, both approaches give learners multiple incidences with retrieving the words and their meaning from their long-term memories. Table 4.5 contains examples of easy-to-implement techniques that increase students' exposure to words used in the context of academic language.

Table 4.5 • Routines for Building Academic Language

TECHNIQUE	DEFINITION	EXAMPLE
Barrier activity	One partner has a picture or information that the other partner does not have. Students sit back-to-back or have a visual obstruction to block their view (a barrier). Using oral language only, students communicate to complete a task.	Tasks may require partners to draw a picture, place objects in specific positions, or find the difference in two pictures. For example, students might describe positions on a map of a battle using directional vocabulary.
Concept sort	Students sort words, phrases, or sentences into categories that relate to the concept they are studying. Sorting may be by category, sequence, characteristics, or another attribute.	Students sort words in a text based on whether the words have positive, neutral, or negative connotations and meaning in order to help them understand mood.
Frayer model cards (Frayer et al., 1969)	Using an index card divided into four quadrants, students (1) name the target word; (2) provide a definition in their own words; (3) identify a word that has the opposite meaning or is a nonexample of the target word; and (4) draw a picture to illustrate it. These are used as personal flashcards.	After developing their own Frayer cards, students practice using target words identified from a text they are reading.

TECHNIQUE	DEFINITION	EXAMPLE
List-group-label (Taba, 1967)	This is a prereading strategy similar to concept sorts, but categories (labels) are developed by the students rather than predetermined. Students brainstorm a *list* of words they expect to encounter in a reading. Then they *group* the words based on similarities. Finally, they develop the *labels* for the groups.	In advance of a reading about the War of 1812, students list words they expect to read, then sort them based on similar features, and finally title the emerging categories.
Word maps	Word maps are another way to build initial understanding as well as depth of knowledge around a concept. As students explore what a word is, what a word is like, and examples (and nonexamples) of the idea or concept, they are strengthening their schema for what a word is by talking and writing. Students add to the word map as they gain more information, clarify their understanding, and connect ideas.	*What is it?* / *What is it like?* — **Kinetic Energy** — *What are some examples?*
Conversation roundtable	After students learn a word or robust concept, they jot down their own thoughts about the word: the definition, examples, nonexamples, and use in sentences. After learners brainstorm their own ideas, they meet with three different partners to hear how others are understanding the word. Then they jot down the new perspectives and decide if they agree or disagree with the examples and usage.	My thoughts / What ____ said / **Target Vocabulary Word** / What ____ said / What ____ said

Hexagonal Thinking

Popularized in the business world, hexagonal thinking is a visual way to help students understand and connect vocabulary words. It involves using hexagon-shaped cards with words or concepts written on them to create a network of connections. (See Table 4.6 for an example of hexagonal thinking.) Here's how you can use this tool with your students.

1. Choose a set of vocabulary words you want students to learn for a unit. Write each word on a hexagon-shaped card. You can start off with a

Video 4.6
Hexagonal Thinking
qrs.ly/7pfya5h

small subset of words initially and add words as the unit progresses, or you can see how students relate unknown words initially.

2. Explain the concept of hexagonal thinking to the students. Let them know they will be using hexagons to make connections between the vocabulary words.

3. Choose a word hexagon to start. Ask students to begin connecting words that are related and to explain their thinking in the process orally or in writing.

4. Invite students to continue building connections by adding additional words and discussing why certain words are connected. They can refine and adjust connections as needed.

5. Have students reflect on their learning and how the routine helped them understand vocabulary.

Table 4.6 • Hexagonal Thinking in Life Sciences

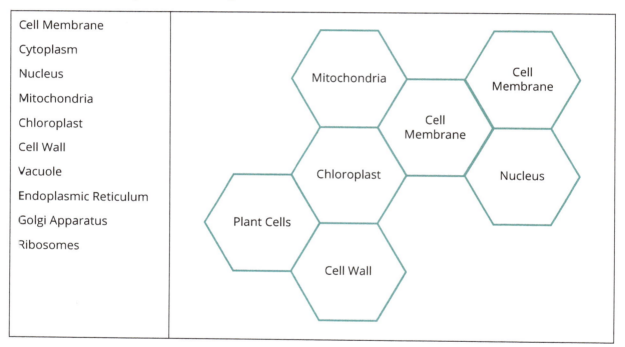

Affinity Mapping

Affinity mapping is a collaborative and visual task used to organize ideas, concepts, or, in this case, vocabulary words based on their similarities. This activity can be done as a whole class, in small groups, or individually throughout a unit so students can see how their thinking has grown and changed to develop deeper understandings of words. Affinity mapping requires students to group like words and concepts based on their relationships; the closer a word is to another word, the stronger the connection. Teachers can use affinity mapping in a variety of ways to get students thinking and talking about words and the relationship between words as they develop unique categories and patterns. Here are the steps you can follow to use affinity mapping with your students:

1. Collect a set of vocabulary words and ask your students to write the words on index cards or sticky notes. (They can also use Google Slides and Jamboards to create the words.)
2. Ask students to silently review the words and pose any questions they might have.
3. Have students work collaboratively to create affinity maps, grouping like words and explaining their decisions.
4. Ask students to name the categories or groupings and to explain the relationships they have determined.
5. Allow students to make adjustments as needed.

This process requires students to select words that are similar and different and to organize the words in meaningful ways. There is not a singular correct map or path. Although students might have erroneous thinking around words, your goal is to hear your students' thinking and their justifications as they develop deeper mental models for what a word is and what it means.

Word Walls

Word walls are not new in education, but how we use them affects their impact. A word wall is a classroom teaching tool used to display and reinforce key vocabulary words, sight words, or subject-specific terminology. It is both a visible and an interactive resource that helps students build their vocabulary and develop their language skills. However, if word walls are simply treated as a visual display with no interaction, their function is lost. Here are a few creative ways to help students use your word wall for more meaningful encounters with words:

- **Word(s) of the day:** Highlight a "word of the day" from the word wall. Encourage students to use that word in their conversations and written work throughout the day. This helps reinforce vocabulary retention.

- **Student-generated word wall:** Allow students to contribute new words to the word wall as they encounter them in their reading or research. This empowers them to take ownership of their vocabulary development.

- **Co-construction:** Work with students to co-construct word walls with definitions in student-friendly language. This exposes students to the academic definitions while allowing them to actively process the words and anchor them with language that is accessible and comprehensible to them.

- **Brain dump:** Choose a few words to call out from the word wall and give students one minute to write down everything they know about the word. For example, if you call out the word *parabola*, students could write the definition, draw a picture, explain the symmetry, write real-world examples, and explain how to determine what direction the parabola opens. This allows for retrieval practice to see what has stuck with students and where they need a little more support.

Classroom Practice: Teaching Word-Learning Strategies

Students require a range of reading strategies to navigate a complex text. By equipping students with a variety of skills, we empower them to choose the appropriate tool needed for the specific struggle they encounter. Word-learning strategies go beyond the teaching of individual words; word meaning can be found both inside the word (morphology) and outside of the word (context). Fisher and Frey (2023) organized word-solving strategies into three components: context clues, morphology and word parts, and resources, which can be represented by the following three-part model:

- **Looking outside the word for contextual clues.** This can include direct definitions or synonyms, the use of punctuation to embed definitions, restatements, contracts, inferences, or explanations.

- **Looking inside the word for structural clues.** Teach prefixes, suffixes, and roots and intentionally explain and model how the use of these word parts helps readers understand new words.

- **Looking outside the word to consult resources.** When necessary, students can use peers, dictionaries, or search engines to help create meaning and context for an unfamiliar word.

When students understand the role of context clues, word families, and how prefixes, suffixes, and roots can help readers understand words, they are better prepared with strategies for attacking new and unfamiliar words. Their use of these strategies improves their word learning because it develops their word-solving strategies.

Voices From the Field

Understanding Greek and Latin roots can help students decode words and understand their meaning. For example, the students in Mr. Campbell's seventh-grade social studies class, who were engaged in a unit about women's history, read the following sentence in an article about Ella McDannel, a trained nurse who worked for a wealthy family at the turn of the 20th century: *The text served as a chronicle of her experiences*

CHAPTER 4 • Word Knowledge

as a domestic servant. To model morphological awareness for students, Mr. Campbell discussed the meaning of *chron-* and its Greek origins, and one student shared that they thought *chronicle* meant that the text was a timeline of the woman's life. Table 4.7 shows an example of a student's organizer.

Table 4.7 • Graphic Organizer in Social Studies

Root: *Chron-* *Chrono-*	Examples and Definitions: • *Chronicle* (historical events in order by time)
Meaning: Time	• *Chronological* (in order by time) • *Chronic* (lasting a long time) • *Synchronize* (at the same time)
Doodle: 	Sentence: I'm always amazed at synchronized swimming during the Olympics because the swimmers dance together in the water, performing the same movements at the same time.

"I teach tenth-grade English," said Jonah Campbell, "and Mr. Walsh teaches math. The students know that when Mr. Walsh explains the etymology of a word or gives meaning to a root word in this class, sometime soon there will be a word in our literature that will allow them to apply what he taught them. The students are always on the lookout and see it as a challenge. For example, in math he introduced the Latin root *numerus*. He explained that there are many words in math connected to this root, like *numeral*, *numerator*, or *numeration*."

The English teacher continued, "About a week later, while we were reading *The Great Gatsby*, one line caught our attention: *When she moved about there was an incessant clicking as innumerable pottery bracelets jingled up and down upon her arms.* Immediately, several students jumped up because they spotted the root word in the word *innumerable*. It's a fun tradition we have, and it is great for students to see that their teachers collaborate with each other and that understanding root words has applicability in various content areas."

Biology teacher Serena Mills-Boyd noticed the need for explicit vocabulary instruction for her advanced placement students. Although many were performing well on tests, she observed that their superficial knowledge of vocabulary limited the students' depth of understanding of complex topics. She decided to implement a "biology term of the day" graphic organizer (Table 4.8) for students to collect a bank of teacher-selected new and necessary words. Using this approach, she asked students to write down a word, draw a picture, paraphrase the definition, and make connections.

Table 4.8 • Term of the Day Graphic Organizer

Word *Antibiotic resistance*	**Picture**
Definition When bacteria develop the ability to survive against antibiotics designed to kill them or stop their growth	
Connections What happens if we develop resistance to modern medicine like penicillin? Could that be deadly for the entire population if a strand of bacteria mutates?	

Word *Microorganism* or *microbe*	**Picture**
Definition Any organism too small to be seen without a microscope	
Connections *Micro* means really small, so it makes sense that *microorganism* is something so small that we need a microscope to see it. Also, *microscope*, which I imagine comes from small (*micro*) and see (*scope*).	

Mrs. Mills-Boyd chose terms of the day like *antibiotic resistance*, *pathogen*, *virus*, and *microorganism/microbe*. Students had multiple opportunities to interact with the word through writing, creating definitions, drawing, and making connections. As students read about the words of the day throughout the unit, they jotted down personal and text connections to the word until they felt they had a strong understanding of the term and it was no longer necessary to study it. When students engage in heightened word consciousness, rehearsal, connections, and retrieval, it helps them create both depth and breadth of knowledge around their new words.

Take Charge: Conclusion and Reflective Questions

For learners in our classrooms, understanding vocabulary involves more than just memorizing definitions; both the breadth and depth of vocabulary knowledge contributes to comprehending and learning from complex texts. Some words can be directly taught, but we must also explicitly model and teach learners how to look inside and outside a word to understand unfamiliar words.

Morphological awareness plays a pivotal role in engaging reading comprehension and vocabulary acquisition among adolescent readers. The smallest parts of words equip readers with clues to uncover the meaning of new words. Given the sheer impracticality of teaching all words, educators can instead focus on teaching affixes and roots, especially those of Greek and Latin origin, to empower students to decipher complex words by recognizing their structural clues. This chapter also advocates for strategies that require active learning methods such as word games, graphic organizers, and word history and connections to help students develop a deeper understanding of language structures.

Vocabulary knowledge is important for reading comprehension; however, vocabulary knowledge alone is unlikely to significantly improve reading comprehension. To help secondary readers make meaningful gains, teachers should pair vocabulary instruction with other language components and content knowledge; this approach is necessary for sizable increases in comprehension to occur (Petscher et al., 2020).

- Think about your next instructional unit and the major terms and vocabulary within the unit. What are the roots within those words that support understanding of those words and that could be transferable to related words?

- The depth and breadth of vocabulary is critical for reading comprehension, and we know it's impossible to teach all words that students will encounter in texts. How will you determine which words are the most crucial for students to know in your discipline?

- Understanding stems, roots, prefixes, and suffixes helps students make sense of newly encountered multisyllabic words. Are there any affixes that are crucial to your content that students need to learn?

- If we aren't careful, vocabulary teaching and learning can turn into a series of dry lesson plans with the goal of memorization. How might you design lessons that integrate vocabulary teaching to support quick wins with students so they can see the benefit of their word learning?

- Teaching too many vocabulary words up front can be overwhelming and result in little to no transfer. How might you scaffold both the introduction and use of newly acquired vocabulary?

- Rehearsal and practice are how learners transfer information into long-term memory. What are some of the aforementioned strategies that you can use in your class to be both intentional and efficient in providing opportunities for students to utilize new vocabulary?

CHAPTER 5

Sentence Analysis
Unlocking the Structure of Language

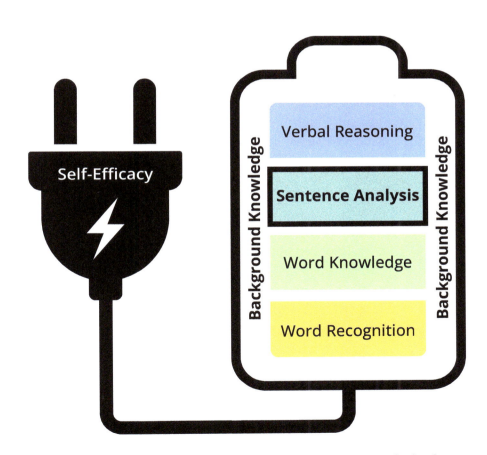

Consider the following four seemingly unrelated words: *butterfly*, *birth*, *technology*, and *galaxy*. Individually, these words each hold meaning, but to convey a coherent message we must arrange and structure them within a sentence, such as the following: *In the study of astronomy, scientists often*

used technology like the Hubble Space Telescope to capture breathtaking images of distant galaxies, butterfly-shaped nebulae, and the birth and death of stars. Although each word contributes to the sentence's meaning, it is the arrangement of these words that conveys thoughts. Fish (2012) put it this way:

> Before the words slide into their slots, they are just discrete items, pointing everywhere and nowhere. Once the words are nested in the places "ordained" for them—*ordained* is a wonderful word that points to the inexorable logic of syntactic structures—they are tied by ligatures of relationships to one another. They are subjects or objects or actions or descriptives or indicators of manner, and as such they combine into a statement about the word, that is into a meaning that one can contemplate, admire, reject, or refine. (p. 2)

Meaning lies within a single sentence as well as across sentences, a characteristic called *sentence cohesion*. For example, read these two sentences:

> The Earth's water cycle, also known as the *hydrological cycle*, involves the continuous movement of water between the Earth's surface, the atmosphere, and back again. During evaporation, water from bodies of water such as oceans, lakes, and rivers is heated by the sun, turning into water vapor and rising into the atmosphere.

In these sentences, the information about the Earth's water cycle in the first sentence provides the context for understanding the process of evaporation described in the second sentence. Although the sentences are dense with concepts, the cohesion between the sentences ties ideas from the first sentence to the second. The reader uses knowledge presented in the first sentence to understand how evaporation fits into the larger cycle of water movement on Earth.

With that in mind, sentence-level instruction is often overlooked in the classroom, even though our students' inability to make connections may be a cause of their poor reading comprehension. As Balthazar and Scott (2024) state, the "inability to comprehend key sentences in a text will undermine finding the main idea, drawing conclusions, making inferences, or answering many comprehension questions" (p. 574). The researchers further quote Shanahan (2022), who notes that "the lowly sentence gets short shrift in most programs and classrooms." Teaching learners to focus on meaning at the sentence and multisentence levels is essential for promoting adolescent reading comprehension.

Let's build our own background knowledge as educators by attending to research findings that underscore the significance of comprehension at the sentence level. Learning to parse sentences and dig into their meaning is a critical skill for adolescents to develop. A key to reading longer pieces of text is the need to understand them sentence by sentence.

Plug Into the Research

Understanding vocabulary and the concepts words represent is undoubtedly important. **Good readers need sophisticated knowledge about the workings of language to make sense of texts.** However, comprehending a text involves more than reading and understanding individual words. At work within sentence structures is grammar. All languages have a grammar, which is the set of rules for the language. Grammar includes the parts of speech (noun, verb, adjective, and so on), as well as the morphology, phonology, and syntax. The large meta-analysis on writing instruction for grades 6–12 found that grammar instruction is an important component for improving writing (Graham et al., 2023).

Syntax is the arrangement of words, phrases, and clauses that form sentences. Comprehension is more complex than simply recognizing individual words and their associated meanings; it requires the ability to make meaning within and across sentences, integrating background knowledge to make sense of the text as a whole. Therefore, our students' ability to understand, produce, and manipulate different sentence structures significantly impacts their reading comprehension (Brimo et al., 2017).

The complexity of phrases and clauses within sentences can undermine comprehension for students with insufficient syntactic awareness. An analysis by Vorstius et al. (2013) revealed notable differences in comprehension accuracy based on the structure of the sentence. For this research, students were asked to read sentences with conjunctions that suggested relationships between clauses. The study found that fifth-grade students demonstrated significantly higher accuracy (83 percent) in understanding sentences with consistent positive information, compared to sentences containing inconsistent negative information (35 percent accuracy).

SYNTAX
arrangement of words, phrases, and clauses that form a sentence

For example, the sentence *Kim smiled because she was happy* was consistent because the first clause (*Kim smiled*) aligned with the second clause (*she was happy*) and was further aligned with the conjunction *because*. In contrast, the sentence *Kim frowned although she was excited* presented greater difficulty in comprehension. The first clause (*Kim frowned*) was not consistent with the second clause (*she was excited*). The relational word *although* highlighted the inconsistency between the two clauses—a much more complex sentence. Sentences such as the second one with the conjunction *although* proved to be more difficult as measured by extended reading times and reduced comprehension.

These comprehension challenges frequently arise from the disparity between students' conversational register—the manner of their speech in daily interactions with their friends—and the more academic "language of schooling" (Schleppegrell, 2001, p. 431). Academic discourse in schools and language in school-based texts have linguistic features that are different from daily spoken language. Table 5.1 outlines some of the notable differences between students' spoken interactions and the language used in school texts.

Table 5.1 • Daily Spoken Language Compared to School Texts Language

LANGUAGE USED IN SPOKEN INTERACTIONS	LANGUAGE USED IN SCHOOL TEXTS
Everyday words	Specialized terminology and academic language
Lower ratio of content words to everyday language within sentences	Higher ratio of content words to everyday language, with sentences dense in technical vocabulary
Subjects of sentences are clearer	Noun phrases and nominalizations (nouns formed from verbs, such as *decide* and *decision*) that make recognizing the subject more complex

Source: Adapted from Schleppegrell (2001).

Fang (2006), who specifically examined features of science-based reading in middle school texts, found several linguistic features that make those texts more complex. In addition to technical vocabulary, which was discussed in the previous chapter, Fang notes multiple examples of challenges faced by adolescent readers as they read science sentences (see Table 5.2).

Table 5.2 • Science Text Language Challenges

SCIENCE TEXT LANGUAGE CHALLENGES	EXAMPLES
Lengthy noun phrases	Chloroplasts, *the organelles within plant cells responsible for photosynthesis*, convert light energy into chemical energy stored in glucose molecules.
Complex sentences	Chemical changes occur when substances react with each other, forming new compounds or breaking down into simpler substances, which can often result in changes in color, temperature, or the release of gas.
Subjects of a sentence separated from the verb and the rest of the sentence	The scientists, under controlled conditions in the laboratory and with meticulous attention to detail, conducted experiments to investigate the effects of varying concentrations of the chemical solution on the rate of reaction.

Source: Adapted from Fang, Z. (2006).

Due to the contrast between language in daily conversations and school texts, students require opportunities to analyze sentences to understand the structures that support their meaning.

Increase Your Battery Life

Students need to develop the ability to understand the structure of sentences because that skill also helps them understand the information in and between sentences. There is a lot to know about teaching students to develop their sentence-level comprehension, but here are some important considerations:

- **Selectively choose sentences, because not every sentence warrants deep analysis.** Focus on sentences that are critical to understanding the content of the subject matter being taught and that warrant investigation because of their complexity.

- **Avoid isolated grammar instruction.** Teaching grammar in isolation, through repetitive worksheets or drills, does not likely translate into improved student reading or writing (Hudson, 2016). And you don't have to be a grammar expert, either. When parsing complex sentences in your content reading, point out how the grammar is used.

- **Prioritize sentence comprehension over grammar terminology.** At the secondary level you can emphasize helping students understand the meaning conveyed by sentences. Instruction with grammar terminology is a plus, but not every content teacher needs to explicitly teach the terminology.

Power Up Classroom Practice

Let's apply the research on sentence-level comprehension to instructional practices that support students' access to content.

- Strategies for analyzing juicy sentences
- Sentence combining
- Crafty sentences
- Close reading

Video 5.1
Juicy Sentences
qrs.ly/2zfya5i

Classroom Practice: Strategies for Analyzing Juicy Sentences

As students are learning to unlock the meaning of a longer text, we can support them by teaching them to analyze one of the sentences that holds key information. This approach, called *juicy sentences,* was originally developed by Fillmore and Fillmore (n.d.) for use with multilingual learners, but it has proven to be effective for all students struggling with comprehending dense text. It requires students, with guidance from the teacher, to read one sentence closely. The routine, which takes only a few minutes, involves deconstructing the selected sentence to unlock its meaning, which primes students for reading the longer text.

Let's use the following sentence from a middle school science course to demonstrate how a teacher can parse a juicy sentence.

> Gradual changes in the shape of Earth's orbit around the Sun (over hundreds of thousands of years), together with the tilt of the planet's spin axis (or axis of rotation), have altered the intensity and distribution of sunlight falling on Earth. (National Academies of Sciences, Engineering, and Medicine, 2012, p. 175)

Using chunks of the sentence, the teacher poses questions to highlight different language structures (see Table 5.3).

The heart of this routine lies in prompting students to engage in class discussion, not in asking students to do this silently and independently. When you use this approach in your classroom, display the juicy sentence on a projector or smartboard and break up the chunks using colors to distinguish the phrases. Point out vocabulary, using morphological awareness as needed. The punctuation and grammar, as well as adverbs and adjectives that modify words, are also good subjects of discussion.

CHAPTER 5 • Sentence Analysis

Table 5.3 • Example of a Juicy Sentence Routine

SENTENCE CHUNK	QUESTIONS TO UNCOVER MEANING
Deconstruct the Sentence	
Gradual changes in the shape of Earth's orbit around the Sun (over hundreds of thousands of years)	The teacher asks, "What does this part of the sentence mean?" After listening to student responses, the teacher may choose to ask more direct questions to prompt the students to make the appropriate connections. Here, the answers appear in brackets: "What is the subject of this part of the sentence?" **[the shape of Earth's orbit around the Sun]** "What does the term *gradual changes* refer to?" **[the shape]** "How long is the time frame over which these changes occur?" **[hundreds of thousands of years]**
together with the tilt of the planet's spin axis (or axis of rotation),	The teacher asks, "What does this part of the sentence mean?" After listening to student responses, the teacher may choose to ask more direct questions to prompt the students to make the appropriate connections. "What is *the planet's spin axis*?" **[it is the axis of rotation]** "What does *tilt* refer to?" **[the axis]** "How does the word *together* tie to the previous chunk?" **[it connects two ideas: the change in the shape of the orbit and the tilt of the axis]**
have altered the intensity and distribution of sunlight falling on Earth.	The teacher asks, "What does this part of the sentence mean?" After listening to student responses, the teacher may choose to ask more direct questions to prompt the students to make the appropriate connections. "What two things have been altered?" **[the sunlight's intensity and the sunlight's distribution]** "Where?" **[in the sunlight that falls on Earth]** "What does it mean for sunlight intensity to be altered?" **[it has changed]**
Reconstruct the Sentence	
Gradual changes in the shape of Earth's orbit around the Sun (over hundreds of thousands of years) + **together with the tilt of the planet's spin axis (or axis of rotation)** = **have altered the intensity and distribution of sunlight falling on Earth.**	The teacher asks students, "What two conditions are discussed?" **[(1) changes to the shape of Earth's orbit and (2) the tilt of Earth's axis]** "What is the effect of these conditions?" **[the intensity and distribution of sunlight has changed]**

Interaction and oral language are key, so use this routine to spark check-ins with small groups before posing questions to the whole class. Otherwise, you may get answers only from students who already know, while learners who may not know sit by passively and silently. After you deconstruct and then reassemble the meaning of the selected sentence, show students where it appears in the longer text. Leverage their newly acquired background knowledge of the selected sentence as a tool for previewing the text as a whole, before they begin to read independently.

Selecting a Juicy Sentence

Not all sentences are worthy of this level of analysis. Consider this advice, adapted from Student Achievement Partners (n.d.), when making decisions about a possible juicy sentence (Table 5.4). Keep in mind that not all criteria must be met for the sentence to be worthy.

Table 5.4 • Selection Criteria for a Juicy Sentence

Comes from grade-appropriate text
Comes from a text that is conceptually connected to content being discussed in class already. This allows students to build on and reinforce the knowledge and vocabulary they've acquired from other texts.
Has high information density. That is, multiple pieces of information are contained in the sentence and/or can be construed from its subtext.
Is "chunkable." You can break it apart into smaller sections for focused discussion. Think strategically about the ideas each chunk is conveying; don't leave students hanging by splitting apart an idea into two chunks.
Features language related to complex thought, where readers are asked to interpret motivation, rationale, time, place, contingencies related to action, etc.
Contains complex noun phrases (nouns that are modified or expanded by other phrases) or adverbial clauses (a group of words that function as an adverb and answer where, when, how, and why)
Uses passive voice (sentences in the passive, rather than active voice, are often harder to comprehend)
Includes linking phrases
Introduces a metaphor or simile

Source: Juicy sentence guidance. Student Achievement Partners. https://achievethecore.org/content/upload/Juicy%20Sentence%20Guidance.pdf

Video 5.2
Sentence
Combining
qrs.ly/g2fya5l

Classroom Practice: Sentence Combining

Sentence combining is a technique that teaches students to recast a series of "short, syntactically simple sentences into ones that are more varied in terms of style, length and syntactic structure" (Saddler et al., 2018). Think of sentence combining as the opposite of juicy sentences. With juicy sentences,

CHAPTER 5 • Sentence Analysis

we disassemble a complex sentence by breaking it into parts. With sentence combining, we assemble several simple sentences to form one complex sentence. This approach supports students in deepening their understanding of course material and learning how to structure and restructure more complex sentences.

To use this approach with your students, select and present three or four related sentences. Then facilitate your students' collaborative efforts to combine the sentences. Your students can share the crafted sentences with their peers, and you can use class discussion to help learners determine if the original meaning of the sentences was preserved. Table 5.5 shows examples of sentences and potential combined sentences.

Table 5.5 • Examples of Sentences in Various Content Areas, and the Combined Version of Those Sentences

INDIVIDUAL SENTENCES FROM CONTENT AREAS	EXAMPLE OF COMBINED SENTENCE
Social Studies	
• During the Renaissance period, artists experimented with new techniques and mediums. • Leonardo da Vinci was one such artist. • He is famous for his masterpiece the *Mona Lisa*. • The *Mona Lisa* is admired for its mysterious smile and realistic portrayal.	During the Renaissance period, artists like Leonardo da Vinci experimented with new techniques and mediums, producing masterpieces such as the *Mona Lisa*, admired for its mysterious smile and realistic portrayal.
Math	
• The Pythagorean theorem is used to find the length of the sides of a right triangle. • It states that the square of the length of the hypotenuse is equal to the sum of the squares of the lengths of the other two sides. • This theorem is named after the ancient Greek mathematician Pythagoras. • He is credited with its discovery and proof.	The Pythagorean theorem, named after the ancient Greek mathematician Pythagoras, who discovered it, is used to find the lengths of the sides of a right triangle by stating that the square of the length of the hypotenuse is equal to the sum of the squares of the lengths of the other two sides.
Health and Nutrition	
• Regular exercise has numerous benefits. • Exercise helps physical and mental health. • Exercise can improve cardiovascular health. • Exercise can strengthen muscles. • Exercise can help you maintain a healthy weight. • Exercise can release endorphins. • Endorphins can reduce stress and improve mood.	Regular exercise has many benefits for physical and mental health, including improving cardiovascular health, strengthening muscles, helping maintain a healthy weight, and releasing endorphins, which can reduce stress and improve mood.

Video 5.3
Crafty Sentences
qrs.ly/qbfya5n

Classroom Practice: Generative Sentences

The use of generative sentences in the classroom offers several benefits (Fearn & Farnan, 2001; Fisher & Frey, 2007):

- It offers students opportunities to skillfully craft sentences.
- Students are continuing to consolidate their knowledge of vocabulary terms.
- Educators can quickly assess students' grasp of the vocabulary and syntax.

To begin, teachers present students with vocabulary terms from their unit, along with specific conditions dictating the structure of each sentence. For instance, conditions for sentences can include limiting the sentence length and the position of the word within the sentence, such that students must consider both the semantic and syntactic conditions.

As an example, sixth-grade science teacher Muhammed Mekel's students were learning about the scientific use of the word *phenomenon* (an event that can be observed with the senses). However, they kept confusing the word with its more generic cousin, *phenomenal* (something extraordinary). To further clarify, Mr. Mekel set a condition using generative sentences by asking them to write a sentence between six to ten words in length, using the word *phenomenon* in the last position. He clarified the task further by saying, "It needs to meet the scientific definition, meaning that it is an observable fact." His students composed and discussed several examples:

- The formation of a rainbow is an example of phenomenon.
- An earthquake is a scientific phenomenon.
- Contagious yawning in people is an observable phenomenon.

Teachers can also design generative sentences to highlight how punctuation impacts sentence patterning. Zena Kendall, a ninth-grade health and nutrition teacher, found that some of her students were struggling to comprehend parenthetical phrases as they read a passage from their textbook about diabetes. She paused the reading and provided some short instruction on parenthetical phrases, then asked the class to construct a sentence containing a parenthetical expression with the noun phrase *blood glucose* in the first position. Working in table groups, the students developed several example sentences, including these:

- Blood glucose levels (measured in milligrams) can change throughout the day.
- Blood glucose (a measure for diabetes) should be below ninety-nine milligrams.
- Blood glucose (the amount of glucose circulating in your blood) is measured after fasting to see if a person is prediabetic.

CHAPTER 5 • Sentence Analysis

Table 5.6 provides prompts for various conditions and offers examples in different content areas.

Table 5.6 • Prompts and Examples for Generative Sentences

Word position	Create a sentence with the word _____ in the _____ position.
	For a math class: Write a sentence that is at least ten words in length with the word *variable* in the ninth position. (Example: *The teacher showed the students how to understand* variables *by saying it is a symbol or letter that takes the place of a number.*)
Word limiters	Provide a range for sentence length: Write a sentence that is between _____ and _____ words in length.
	Provide a minimum length (e.g., at least seven words).
	Provide a maximum length (e.g., no more than fifteen words).
	Provide a specific length (e.g., exactly eleven words).
	For a fire technology class: Write a sentence that is exactly fifteen words and includes the word *acute*. (Example: *In our EMT class, we learn how to recognize and respond to* acute *medical emergencies.*)
Sentence patterning (punctuation)	Write a sentence with an independent clause and a semicolon.
	Use a colon with a list.
	Include a parenthetical expression in a sentence.
	For a psychology class: Write a sentence that includes the word *amygdala* and also contains a colon. (Example: *The* amygdala *helps to do the following: regulate emotions, process memories, and control fear.*)
Sentence structure	Use the conjunction *although*.
	Begin the sentence with a dependent clause.
	For a government and economics class: Use the word *commerce* in a sentence that has a dependent clause. (Example: *While* commerce *includes trade and money transactions, it also helps connect the global economy.*)

Classroom Practice: Close Reading

Close reading is a practice that engages students in multiple readings of a complex text, paired with questions that lead into a deeper understanding. Teachers frame this approach with discussion, using text-dependent questions that cause students to return time and again to the text to unlock meaning. While learners can practice close reading on longer pieces of text, we find it especially useful at the paragraph level with paragraphs chosen from a longer reading. The purpose of this multisentence-level instruction is to fuel the learners' deeper understanding of a dense passage so they can further unlock the larger reading.

Video 5.4
Close Reading
qrs.ly/irfya5p

Text selection is an important component, as the decision to devote ten to fifteen minutes of instructional time to allow students to unpack the meaning of several paragraphs should not be taken lightly. When selecting text, educators should think critically about what makes that text complex (Fisher & Frey, 2014); this understanding helps us craft questions that prompt our students to dig deeper into the meaning of the text and its connections to other readings. You can use Table 5.7 as a guide to consider the aspects of various literary components that could pose a challenge to readers.

Table 5.7 • Qualitative Factors of Text Complexity

COMPONENT	ASPECTS	WHEN A TEXT IS COMPLEX . . .
Levels of meaning and purpose	Density and complexity	Many ideas come at the reader, or there are multiple levels of meaning, some of which are not clearly stated.
	Figurative language	There are many literary devices (e.g., metaphors, personification) or devices that the reader is not familiar with (e.g., symbolism, irony) as well as idioms or clichés.
	Purpose	Either the purpose is not stated or is purposefully withheld. The reader has to determine the theme or message.
Structure	Genre	The genre is unfamiliar or the author bends the rules of the genre.
	Organization	It does not follow traditional structures such as problem/solution, cause/effect, compare/contrast, sequence or chronology, and rich descriptions.
	Narration	The narrator is unreliable, changes during the course of the text, or has a limited perspective for the reader.
	Text features	Fewer signposts such as headings, bold words, margin notes, font changes, or footnotes are used.
	Graphics	Visual information is not repeated in the text itself, but the graphics or illustrations are essential to understanding the main ideas.
Language conventionality and clarity	Standard English and variations	Variations of standard English, such as regional dialects or vernaculars that the reader is not familiar with, are included.
	Register	It is archaic, formal, scholarly, or fixed in time.
Knowledge demands	Background knowledge	The demands on the reader extend well beyond the reader's personal life experience.
	Prior knowledge	The demands on the reader extend well beyond what the reader has been formally taught in school.
	Cultural knowledge	The demands on the reader extend well beyond the reader's cultural experiences and may include references to archaic or historical cultures.
	Vocabulary	The words used are representations of complex ideas that are unfamiliar to the reader or they are domain specific and not easily understood using context clues or morphological knowledge.

Source: Frey, N., & Fisher, D. (2013).

As we've noted, several conditions are inherent to the close-reading process, including annotating text and discussion propelled by text-dependent questions (Fisher & Frey, 2014). Teachers can help learners read the text closely by prompting them to use these three main annotation schemes:

- Underlining central ideas
- Circling words and phrases that are confusing
- Writing margin notes in their own words

The simplicity of this annotation routine is particularly helpful for students. For teachers, it also doesn't require you to provide a page of different possible annotation marks you need to teach and constantly review. Instead, this approach encourages students to identify the most important ideas, self-monitor their comprehension, and write short phrases to help them cognitively hold on to those important ideas. In turn, these text mark-ups allow teachers to monitor what the learners are understanding and what they are finding to be confusing.

The power of close reading stems from multiple readings and discussions of this short piece of text. The teacher asks carefully crafted questions that scaffold students' understanding of the paragraph by moving their thinking from a more literal understanding to a more inferential one. Questions are grouped into four phases (Fisher & Frey, 2014):

1. What does the text say?
2. How does the text work?
3. What does the text mean?
4. What does the text inspire you to do?

Let's briefly examine each phase in more detail.

What does the text say? These questions ensure that students grasp the overall view of the text. Often these are global questions that require students to demonstrate an understanding of what the author really said. Depending on the type of text, these questions may probe the sequence of information presented, the story arc, the main claim and evidence presented, or the gist of a given passage.

How does the text work? Questions in this phase focus students' attention on the vocabulary used as well as on the writer's word choice decisions. Other questions in this phase highlight the structural and organizational means used in the text. Common organizational structures at the secondary level include claims, evidence, and reasoning in argumentative texts and expository devices such as cause/effect, problem/solution, and compare/contrast.

What does the text mean? Questions that probe the deeper meaning of the passage encourage students to make inferences. Inferences involve more than asking students to make guesses or simply telling students to "read between the lines." Readers need to know how to probe each argument in persuasive text, each idea in informational text, and each key detail in literary text; they also need to know how to observe the ways these arguments build to a whole. Text-dependent questions should prompt students to consider the information that is provided and then make informed interpretations.

What does the text inspire you to do? This is the agentic question, which is meant to tap into students' motivation and interest. In many cases, this question is intended to introduce a question that students can answer only through further reading of the longer text. In other cases, the question may be a call to make connections to previous learning, or to spark investigation.

Developing text-dependent questions can be labor intensive. However, with the advent of artificial intelligence tools, teachers can easily generate draft questions to refine for close-reading discussion. As an example, here's how we used MagicSchool.ai (https://app.magicschool.ai/tools) to generate text-dependent questions for a passage from a chapter used in a ninth-grade ethnic studies class.

First, we pasted the passage into the text-dependent question generator feature:

> When it was clear that there was no gold left, the Indians were enslaved on the Spaniards' huge estates. They were overworked and mistreated, and they died by the thousands. By 1550, only five hundred Indians remained. A century later, no Arawaks were left on the island. (Zinn, 2023, p. 10)

Then we set the grade level and prompted the AI tool to provide questions at the literal, structural, and interpretive levels, asking for three possible questions for each level. We reviewed the questions and selected one at each level:

- *What does the text say?* What happened to the Indians on the Spaniards' estates when it was evident there was no more gold?

- *How does the text work?* In what way does the abrupt transition from discussing the enslaved Indians to the complete disappearance of the Arawaks contribute to the overall impact of the passage?

- *What does the text mean?* What conclusions can you draw about what the Spaniards valued and what they did not?

One of the questions generated was not text dependent, but we recognized that it could be used to fuel further reading of the chapter by setting a purpose for inquiry: *Were there any instances of resistance or attempts by the Arawaks to fight against their mistreatment on the Spaniards' estates?* Drawing on what students know and do not know (but are curious to learn more about) is a great way to motivate them to persist in reading complex texts.

Voices From the Field

Jeremy Nguyen's class was immersed in the unit "Understanding Power and Power Structures" in their tenth-grade English course. They were working to define power and discuss its significance in society. The teacher integrated a variety of other sources for students to get a fuller understanding of the concept of power in the United States and its representations in narrative and expository texts.

Mr. Nguyen routinely used the close-reading strategy for students to analyze various texts, and in one lesson, he invited students to read the following five-sentence paragraph from Luis Rodriguez's memoir, *Always Running: Mi Vida Loca* (2005):

> We didn't call ourselves gangs. We called ourselves clubs or *clicas*. In the back lot of the local elementary school, about a year after Tino's death, five of us gathered in the grass and created a club—"Thee Impersonations," the "Thee" being an old English usage that other clubs would adopt because it made everything sound classier, nobler, *badder*. It was something to belong to—something that was ours. We weren't in boy scouts, in sports teams or camping groups. Thee Impersonations is how we wove something out of the threads of nothing. (p. 41)

Table 5.8 outlines the questions that Mr. Nguyen asked during the close-reading activity. Initially, students collaborated in groups on a question, which then led to a whole class discussion. Mr. Nguyen used the first questions to check for general understanding, but then he allowed for longer and more in-depth discussion in the latter questions. The second column includes a brief summary of some of the points and comments made by students.

Notice how the questions evolve. Mr. Nguyen's initial questions ensure that students first have a literal understanding of the text. Then he moves to questions that invite analysis at the structural level. Eventually, his questions cause students to consider the deeper meaning; this step occurs before he

Table 5.8 • Four Phases of Close-Reading Questions

TEXT-DEPENDENT QUESTIONS	SUMMARY OF POINTS MADE BY CLASS
What does the text say? What is that paragraph mostly about?	The paragraph mainly spoke of how Luis and his friends started the club, Thee Impersonations.
How does the text work? Reread this sentence: "In the back lot of the local elementary school, about a year after Tino's death, five of us gathered in the grass and created a club—'Thee Impersonations,' the 'Thee' being an old English usage that other clubs would adopt because it made everything sound classier, nobler, *badder*." Why is the last word italicized? How does the use of three comparative adjectives at the end of that sentence contribute to the narrator's reasoning behind the creation of their club?	The narrator, Luis, is making the point that the addition of the word *thee* brings more prestige to the group. The words *classier* and *nobler* signify that the groups are a positive influence and people should feel proud to be a part of them. The last word, *badder*, is italicized and the author is definitely wanting the reader to see that it is different from the other two words. *Badder* almost seems like the opposite of those words. But all of them have *-er* at the end, as if this group is compared to something else. We think they are comparing their group to other groups, but maybe they want to be tougher than other groups.
What does the text mean? Reread the first two sentences of that paragraph. What is the significance of the labels being used?	In the first sentence, the author uses *gangs* as the label for these groups. But the group members themselves don't identify with being in a gang. They use *clubs* or *clicas*. It seems like the society outside of this culture wants to label them with something that is negative. But Luis is saying they are just as valid as a camping group.
What does the text mean? Reread the paragraphs from yesterday's reading. How do the narrator's first experience in school and this paragraph on the creation of clubs connect to the concept of power?	In yesterday's reading, Luis was isolated from the class because his teacher didn't think he was intelligent because he didn't speak English. The narrator even said that using Spanish was a punishable offense. So that means that people who spoke another language were seen as less intelligent, and also possibly as a threat. Luis felt disconnected from school. I think he felt powerless, or less than. In today's reading, I could see that the creation of this club helped him feel like he belonged. It helped him feel like he was worthy. Luis even uses the words *nobler* and *classier* with the addition of *thee* to his club's name. Then he uses *badder* to signify a sense of power.
What does this text inspire you to do? What does this text inspire you to want to learn more about within this unit of study?	Our group said they never thought about how a need for a sense of power might affect the actions of a group of people or a culture. They wanted to know more about how marginalized groups have responded, and they wanted to know which actions have proven to be more successful.

introduces an agentic question. The sequence of the questions themselves serves as a scaffold to deeper understanding—both of the text and also of connections to concepts beyond the text.

Take Charge: Conclusion and Reflective Questions

Understanding how sentences are structured and connected is vital for comprehending complex-content texts. As educators, we can teach students to infer relationships and draw conclusions based on contextual cues embedded within the text. By prioritizing sentence comprehension over grammar terminology and by providing opportunities for sentence analysis in the classroom, teachers can empower students to navigate texts more thoughtfully and effectively.

- Incorporating sentence analysis into classroom instruction can improve students' reading skills and their understanding of content. How might you incorporate sentence-analysis activities into your lesson plans?

- Sentence-combining activities can improve learners' content knowledge and writing skills by manipulating clauses and phrases. What sentences can you provide students with that will help them consolidate information in your content area and also allow them to combine sentences?

- Close reading of paragraphs allows students to understand how the sentences are connected together to convey meaning. How can you create a routine for close reading of paragraphs in your content classes?

CHAPTER 6

Verbal Reasoning
Thinking With Words Across Texts

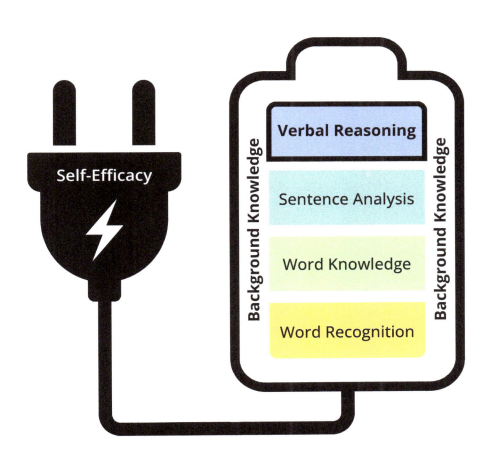

Readers use verbal reasoning to understand what's happening in written and spoken language. We ask you to read this paragraph from Wikipedia on the Haitian Revolution (2024) and then we will point out some of the ways you used verbal reasoning to understand the text:

The Haitian Revolution was a successful insurrection by self-liberated slaves against French colonial rule in Saint-Domingue, now the sovereign state of Haiti.

The revolt began on 22 August 1791, and ended in 1804 with the former colony's independence. It involved Black, biracial, French, Spanish, British, and Polish participants—with the ex-slave Toussaint Louverture emerging as Haiti's most prominent general. The revolution was the only slave uprising that led to the founding of a state which was both free from slavery (though not from forced labour) and ruled by non-whites and former captives. The successful revolution was a defining moment in the history of the Atlantic World and the revolution's effects on the institution of slavery were felt throughout the Americas. The end of French rule and the abolition of slavery in the former colony was followed by a successful defense of the freedoms the former slaves had won, and with the collaboration of already free people of color, of their independence from white Europeans.

As you read this entry, which is filled with vocabulary and historical concepts, the complex phenomenon of verbal reasoning was taking place both consciously and unconsciously in your mind. Words like *abolition, revolution, slavery,* and *independence* likely have strong enough context in your mind so you didn't have to engage in effortful thinking about what they mean. When the text referenced the *state*, you probably concluded early on that it was the country of Haiti, and when the *colony* was referenced subsequently, you likely determined it was Saint-Domingue. You most likely summarized the big ideas as you read, and the more you knew about the Haitian Revolution, the easier the summary was. More complicated were the ideas that required you to make connections across the text about Toussaint Louverture and the timeline of Haiti abolishing slavery in comparison to the U.S. abolishment of slavery sixty years later.

You may also have questioned why France cared to rule this tiny island and how the formerly enslaved people were able to overthrow French rule under Napoleon Bonaparte's emperorship. These more effortful connections across the text, combined with your background knowledge, required you to remember what happened at the beginning of the text in order to connect it with ideas at the end. You had to build on your prior knowledge, make inferences, connect ideas, and understand implicit meaning to draw conclusions, all the while holding the main ideas in your mind. Reading requires learners to make connections between words, sentences, paragraphs, and pages in a text. All these complex skills, whether effortless or effortful, require verbal reasoning.

Don't let the word *verbal* throw you off: Verbal reasoning is the skill people use to make sense of language, whether spoken or written. But it encompasses more than just comprehension as it requires learners to use all they know to

CHAPTER 6 • Verbal Reasoning

reach conclusions that are logical. We really like this definition, extracted from the work of Bruner and colleagues in 1956: *Reasoning involves going beyond the information given to a more structured and precise understanding* (Burton et al., 2009).

The importance of verbal reasoning in middle and high school cannot be overstated. State standardized tests are composed heavily of questions requiring verbal reasoning, as are national tests like the PSAT/NMSQT, SAT, ACT, GED, and the military entrance exam known as the Armed Services Vocational Aptitude Battery (ASVAB). Beyond testing, verbal reasoning is built into our state standards and used daily in disciplinary content. Here are ten ways verbal reasoning is used in reading:

1. Evaluating the reliability, bias, and credibility of sources in social studies
2. Interpreting emotion in poetry
3. Making connections across sentence and paragraph boundaries
4. Listening to and following directions
5. Recognizing patterns of data
6. Carrying out an experiment with prescribed instructions in science
7. Forming hypotheses based on information

8. Comparing and contrasting viewpoints
9. Analyzing relevant information in word problems in math
10. Understanding figurative language

This list is not exhaustive, but it is meant to show the broad nature of verbal reasoning and the need for developing students' reasoning skills. In this chapter, we will explore ways to increase students' verbal-reasoning abilities to strengthen their ability to understand written and spoken language.

Plug Into the Research

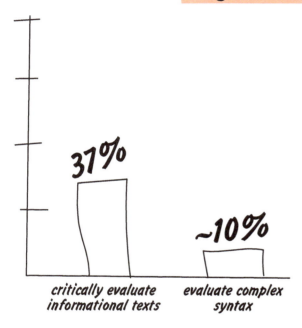

When it comes to learning disciplinary content, the acquisition of new and complex knowledge through hearing or reading relies on verbal reasoning. One longitudinal study (Walston et al., 2008) tracked a nationally representative group of twenty-five thousand U.S. students as they progressed from kindergarten through eighth grade. When the researchers assessed the learners at the end of eighth grade, they found that only 37 percent of the students could critically evaluate and understand informational texts, and less than 10 percent could correctly evaluate complex syntax, both of which are skills that heavily rely on verbal reasoning (Reardon et al., 2012). More recently, a survey conducted by the EdWeek Research Center showed that 94 percent of a nationally representative group of teachers, principals, and district leaders claimed their students struggle with reading comprehension (Sawchuck, 2024). Thus, improving students' abilities to reason is a necessary step in moving learning forward.

Reading comprehension strategies such as making inferences, rereading, annotating, and predicting are often the default approaches that secondary educators use to fix reading gaps by having students monitor their understanding as they connect new ideas. Although comprehension strategies can be helpful for teaching students to monitor their understanding, the strategies cannot exist in isolation. Researchers and literacy experts cite that comprehension strategies help readers think differently about a text, but they do not work when students lack sufficient content knowledge (Elleman, 2017; Rothkopf, 2008).

In fact, a 2023 meta-analysis on the effects of reading strategies on struggling readers' comprehension found the effects of strategies held only when background knowledge instruction was included (Peng et al., 2024). "It is

not 'the more we teach, the better outcomes to expect,'" stated the researchers. "Background knowledge instruction should be combined with strategy instruction to facilitate knowledge retrieval as to reduce the cognitive load of using strategies" (p. 228). If students are to improve their reading abilities, we need to bridge knowledge with strategies to help students understand the reasoning process.

COGNITIVE LOAD: amount of information the brain can process at any given time

The Education Testing Service (ETS), the organization that administers the aforementioned college entrance exams, sought to clarify what exactly is meant by (and measured in) verbal reasoning (Burton et al., 2009). They identified eight dimensions for assessing verbal reasoning, and they proposed a framework for verbal reasoning that encompasses many of the elements already discussed in this book (see Table 6.1). Notably, self-monitoring, while important, is only one of the dimensions in the framework.

Reading comprehension is complex, but **helping students improve their reasoning through multiple approaches can have tremendous payoff** in academic achievement and the learning of disciplinary content (Klauer & Phye, 2008).

Increase Your Battery Life

Knowledge-building is key to development of verbal reasoning skills. Keep these principles in mind to amplify the impact of your teaching:

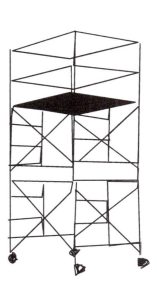

- **Encourage students to read grade-level texts.** Students often learn content through reading, and one of the ways learners get better at reading complex texts is by applying the skills they have been taught in complex texts. When teachers are working with readers who are not yet at expected levels, they can be tempted to avoid grade-appropriate texts altogether because the students will struggle to comprehend them. However, when you use texts with reductions and omissions, you reduce learners' access to the knowledge necessary for verbal reasoning to deepen. Instead, you can scaffold the learners' thinking and allow your students the opportunity to wrestle with concepts, practice synthesizing and making connections, and draw conclusions from complex sentences and structures.

- **Pair comprehension strategies with vocabulary and the building of background knowledge.** Too often educators use comprehension strategies as the sole means to fix comprehension gaps. Strategies require students to have the appropriate vocabulary and background

Teaching Foundational Skills to Adolescent Readers

Table 6.1 • ETS Verbal-Reasoning Framework

DIMENSION	DEFINITION
Understand discourse	Understand the meanings of words, sentences, and entire texts. Understand relationships among words and among concepts, and understand the structure of text. Reason from incomplete data, inferring missing information or connections. Select important points, distinguish major from minor or irrelevant points, summarize. Use different reading strategies, depending on the text and one's purpose in reading; use multiple strategies for remembering.
Interpret discourse	Analyze and draw conclusions from and about discourse. Identify author's/speaker's perspective and assumptions. Understand multiple levels of meaning (such as literal, figurative, author's intent, etc.).
Evaluate discourse	Identify strengths and weaknesses. Raise questions about the implications of discourse. Consider alternative explanations. Understand and balance multiple perspectives. Appraise author's definitions and assumptions, evaluating sources for bias, self-interest, and lack of expertise. Recognize fallacies in argument.
Incorporate discourse with knowledge base and beliefs	Evaluate differences between one's knowledge base and beliefs and discourse; integrate new information into one's knowledge base; revise/reorganize prior knowledge and beliefs based on discourse. This might include discarding ideas that one judges to be wrong, but it might also include retaining knowledge and beliefs that are in conflict in recognition of the value of alternative viewpoints.
Create new understandings	Move beyond the reception of knowledge to the use and application of knowledge. Build upon discourse by integrating, elaborating, and transforming the content. Synthesize information from a variety of sources. Incorporate understanding in a larger framework. Compare, contrast, and integrate perspectives.
Seek and solve problems	Identify areas that require further thought and research. Develop possible explanations, and test them. Apply knowledge and verbal-reasoning strategies to new problem situations. Use verbal-reasoning and self-monitoring skills to set goals, plan, and overcome obstacles in the course of problem solving.
Communicate	Write, present, explain, define, persuade, teach, provide feedback to, and interact with people from a variety of communities of discourse. Become fluent in the language and conventions of one's own discipline.
Monitor one's own comprehension, reasoning, and habits of mind	Use multiple criteria to monitor comprehension while reading; change strategies when comprehension is unsatisfactory. Use multiple strategies for overcoming obstacles in problem solving. Strive to be well-informed, open-minded, flexible, creative; to maintain personal and professional integrity; and to maintain a broad perspective.

Source: Copyright © 2009 by Educational Testing Service. All rights reserved. Used with permission of John Wiley and Sons, from *Toward a definition of verbal reasoning in higher education*, Thomas Essen, Irene Kostin, Cynthia Welsh, et al., 2009; permission conveyed through Copyright Clearance Center, Inc.

knowledge—or else these isolated comprehension strategies won't unlock the meaning of the text. Telling students to "make inferences" and "reread" does little to assist them if they do not have sufficient knowledge. When learners lack the appropriate topical knowledge to complete these tasks, they get frustrated and fail to persist, thereby undermining self-efficacy.

- **Teach critical-thinking skills as students build conceptual knowledge.** Critical thinking is not a set of discrete steps or procedures that students can memorize; it is largely dependent on background knowledge and vocabulary. It is impossible for learners to think critically about ideas they don't know. Make sure your students have relevant appropriate knowledge and embed critical thinking into meaningful reading tasks while providing them with adequate scaffolding and support.

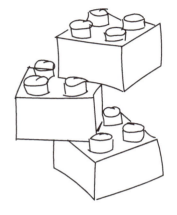

Power Up Classroom Practice

A common practice teachers use with students who have historically struggled with reading comprehension involves giving learners an easier, less complex version of the same text. However, when educators do this, they increase the achievement gaps between lower-performing and higher-performing readers by robbing students of the access to grade-level ideas, which come from increased complexity. Counterintuitively, providing easier versions of texts does not necessarily improve comprehension. A study by Lupo and Torotelli (2017) found that ninth-grade students who were given an easier-to-read text fared similarly on comprehension performance and growth over time as when they read a challenging text. The easier-to-read texts (written at the fifth- or sixth-grade level) contained easier vocabulary, familiar words, simple sentence structure, and conversational tone; the challenging texts (written at the ninth- to twelfth-grade level) contained abstract vocabulary, complex sentence structures, more rare words, and academic vocabulary. Students who had a comprehension level below the national average did not receive an immediate boost in comprehension from reading the easier text nor an improvement in their comprehension ability.

To illustrate, consider the two paragraphs about photosynthesis in Table 6.2. The first is written at a high school equivalency and the second is written for sixth grade.

Table 6.2 • Two Passages About Photosynthesis

HIGH SCHOOL EQUIVALENCY (1410 LEXILE)	SIXTH-GRADE EQUIVALENCY (800 LEXILE)
Photosynthesis is a complex biochemical process fundamental to life on Earth. It occurs in the chloroplasts of plant cells and is essential for converting light energy into chemical energy in the form of glucose. During photosynthesis, plants absorb carbon dioxide from the atmosphere and use the energy from sunlight, captured by chlorophyll pigments, to split water molecules into oxygen and hydrogen ions. The oxygen is released into the air, providing a crucial component for respiration, while the hydrogen ions are used to create adenosine triphosphate (ATP), a molecule that stores and transports energy within the cell. Ultimately, the glucose produced through photosynthesis serves as both an energy source and a building block for plant growth, making it a vital process for sustaining life on our planet.	Photosynthesis is a crucial process for plants. It happens in their cells and uses sunlight to make food. Think of it like a solar-powered factory inside a plant's leaves. Here's how it works: Plants have a green pigment called chlorophyll that captures sunlight. They also take in carbon dioxide from the air and water from the ground. Using sunlight, plants turn these ingredients into sugar and oxygen. The sugar is like plant food, providing energy for the plant to grow. And the oxygen is released into the air, which is good for all of us to breathe. So, photosynthesis is like the plant's way of making its own food and giving us clean air in return.

The first paragraph contains grade-appropriate academic vocabulary for high schoolers, as well as complex sentence structures with modifiers, referents, and determinants. The second contains simple sentences, analogies that help students make sense of the ideas, and familiar words. While the second paragraph has an easier readability, it not only blocks students from accumulating the depth of knowledge required to tackle increasingly complex ideas but also denies them the opportunity to engage with and practice their verbal-reasoning skills. Think of it as a light version of weight training. Lifting the same weight year after year won't harm you, but it won't necessarily make you stronger, either.

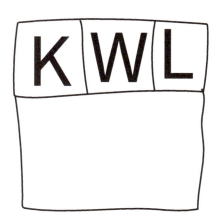

In Chapter 2 on developing background knowledge we discussed the strategy of quad text selection, which offers students an easier text to help them build their background knowledge (Lupo et al., 2020). However, the goal is always for students to apply that knowledge to a challenging text. Even students with a history of low reading achievement can comprehend challenging texts with the right instructional support.

A study of nearly three hundred ninth-grade students over a semester is instructive and enlightening (Lupo et al., 2019). Students read either below-grade-level texts or grade-level texts. Some students experienced a listen-read-discuss routine where the teacher provided a lecture to build background knowledge, followed by independent reading and discussion. Other students experienced the K-W-L routine (Ogle, 1986), which is designed with inquiry and critical thinking in mind. (K-W-L was discussed in Chapter 2 on background knowledge.) Interestingly, students who read either the easier or more challenging texts made progress in the K-W-L lessons, but those who made the most progress read challenging texts *and* participated in K-W-L lessons. The effect of reading challenging texts and engaging in K-W-L accelerated reading achievement for students below, at, or above grade level. The takeaway? When readers have opportunities to engage in verbal reasoning, paired with more complex texts to build knowledge, their reading comprehension gains surged.

The same study included interviews with the participating teachers who discussed their regular instructional practices before the study took place. According to the researchers, most teachers admitted that "instruction for students who read below average typically includes *fewer overall reading encounters, less discussion about texts, and fewer opportunities for students to read texts independently*" (Lupo et al., 2019, p. 475, emphasis added). Further, "The teachers who also taught honors courses stated that they typically provide more opportunities for students in their honors courses to read independently and discuss the text than they do in non-honors classes" (Lupo et al., 2019, p. 475).

Before we continue, though, let's be clear: Throwing developing readers into challenging texts without any support is not helpful, and it will likely lead to frustration and failure. But it's also essential to understand there isn't just one lever that holds the secret to strengthening adolescent reading. To help our students develop solid reading skills, we need to use as many of the most effective tools as we can in harmony with one another. In the examples discussed here, activating knowledge, engaging in verbal reasoning, and using grade-level texts made the difference.

Power Up Classroom Practice

In the next section, we'll explore the following instructional practices, which support students' access to content while promoting their verbal reasoning.

- Promote metacognitive thinking
- Provide explicit instruction to link strategies with knowledge and metacognition
- Use generative learning activities
- Activate dialogue
- Use distributed and front-end scaffolds

Classroom Practice: Promote Metacognitive Thinking

As educators, it is essential that we allow students the opportunity to monitor and own their learning. Pouring knowledge into our students' heads is not how learning works. Learners must cognitively engage to develop understanding. One of the goals of reading comprehension in middle and high school is for students to acquire, consolidate, and deepen their understanding of content.

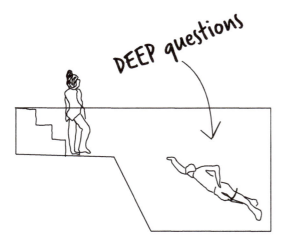

Facts are important. Concepts are important. But the ability to understand and explain the relationship between ideas and further apply them in different contexts is the level of understanding students need in secondary settings. Students need opportunities to think—and to think deeply. If the majority of questions we ask are low-level, fact-oriented questions, then their thinking will remain at the shallow end of the conceptual pool. Instead, we need to ask questions that prompt our students' thinking about connections across texts and concepts, as well as about links to previously learned content.

One way teachers can promote metacognitive thinking is through modeling and questioning. Using a small text excerpt, model the thinking you hope to generate in students and provide metacognitive questions like those in Table 6.3 to support the learners' thinking and awareness of their own learning.

Table 6.3 • Fostering Metacognition Through Reflective Questioning

PLANNING FOR LEARNING	MONITORING LEARNING	REFLECTING ON LEARNING
What do I need to be ready to engage in this lesson (materials, pre-reading, etc.)? Am I prepared to learn? Is my phone put away? What information on this topic do I already know?	What information is the most important to add to my notes? Should I ask for help from my peers? What can I do to get unstuck (by myself, with the help of peers, with the teacher)? What is the most confusing thing about this information or process? Where did I get stuck?	What can I teach others? What are three main points from the lesson? How actively was I involved in the learning? What decisions did I make during learning that were beneficial to my learning? What decisions did I make during learning that did not support my learning?

Classroom Practice: Provide Explicit Instruction to Link Strategies With Knowledge and Metacognition

Verbal reasoning is a means to a larger end, not a set of isolated skills to be learned individually. Purcell-Gates and colleagues (2016) put it this way:

Video 6.1
Metacognition
qrs.ly/msfya5s

> Teaching the many skills involved in the reading process requires teaching the components of a whole. For example, when teaching children to ride a bicycle, we teach them to pedal, to manage speed, to brake, to steer, to balance. We also teach them to coordinate these skills (e.g., to steer while braking). And we teach them how to adjust and even add skills in different contexts (e.g., to manage speed in traffic and on an open road, to use hand signals when the situation demands it). Of course, all these skills are learned in a context of use—a context that is functional and meaningful for the learner (e.g., to travel on a bicycle from place to place for transportation or as a form of play). (p. 1226)

While the reading and reasoning process is not linear, intentional efforts to consolidate the two increase the rate of learning. Students need verbal-reasoning skills, but many learners struggle to create high-quality evaluations and conclusions without explicit instructional support. It's not enough just to tell learners to explain connections, draw conclusions, synthesize ideas, or make inferences. Rather, in our classrooms we should model the thinking needed to accomplish these tasks, and then we can gradually release the verbal-reasoning process to our students.

It's also important to recognize that thinking aloud is not the same as telling. The practice of teacher think-alouds includes the use of "I" statements designed to provide students insight into how and why a particular problem-solving approach is used. Think of your favorite how-to show as an example. The best ones provide the viewer with ongoing commentary from the expert about the following steps:

1. The expert's recognition of a problem

2. The possible solutions the expert considers (and, in some cases, discards)

3. The use of the physical or mental tool the expert used to solve the problem

For instance, during a think-aloud about questioning, the teacher might use wording like this:

> Oops, I noticed the writer made a really strong statement in that last paragraph, and it's one I'm not sure I totally agree with. Already I've stopped reading because I need to think about that claim. I'm rereading it because I want to make sure I fully grasped what the writer is saying. [The teacher rereads.] So now I've got questions I expect the writer to answer. I'm going to jot them down in the margin and come back to them to see if I really did get the answers I was looking for as I continue reading.

When learners have sufficient knowledge, teachers can greatly impact their students' reasoning skills by modeling and thinking aloud about comprehension strategies. When you use think-alouds in your classroom, your explanations of your reasoning further promote your students' metacognitive awareness—their ability to consciously notice and act upon their own thinking (Flavell, 1979). Table 6.4 details reading comprehension strategies related to dimensions of verbal reasoning, with accompanying definitions.

Video 6.2
Summarizing
qrs.ly/lcfya5v

Table 6.4 • Reading Comprehension Strategies for Older Readers

STRATEGY	DEFINITION
Activating	"Priming the cognitive pump" to recall relevant prior knowledge and experiences from long-term memory in order to extract and construct meaning from text
Inferring	Bringing together what is spoken (written) in the text, what is unspoken (unwritten) in the text, and what is already known by the reader to extract and construct meaning from the text
Monitoring/clarifying	Thinking about how and what one is reading, both during and after the act of reading, for purposes of determining if one is comprehending the text combined with the ability to clarify and fix up any mix-ups
Questioning	Engaging in learning dialogues with text (authors), peers, and teachers through self-questioning, question generation, and question answering
Searching/selecting	Searching a variety of sources to select appropriate information to answer questions, define words and terms, clarify misunderstandings, solve problems, or gather information
Summarizing	Restating the meaning of text in one's own words—different words from those used in the original text
Visualizing/organizing	Constructing a mental image or graphic organizer for the purpose of extracting and constructing meaning from the text

Source: McEwan-Adkins, E. K. (2007).

To help students understand these cognitive strategies, start by defining the strategy and explaining why it's helpful. Then, model the use of the strategy to demonstrate the thinking process required of the specific strategy. Allow students time to practice the strategy and reflect on its impact.

Classroom Practice: Generative Learning Activities

Generative strategies have legs; they move learning forward. They make thinking visible because students are required to produce something meaningful and make conscious sense of their learning. In other words, they are required to be metacognitive (Fiorella & Mayer, 2015). Multiple research studies and meta-analyses show that strategies such as concept mapping, explaining, predicting, and drawing are effective for secondary students, all producing strong evidence that these methods accelerate learning (Brod, 2021). In Table 6.5, cognitive scientist and researcher Logan Fiorella (2023) details three types of generative-learning activities.

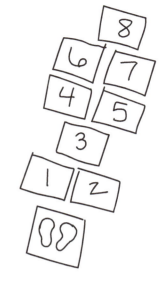

Table 6.5 • Explaining, Visualizing, and Enacting as Generative Learning Activities (GLA)

GLA TYPE	DESCRIPTION	EXAMPLES
Visualizing	Generating coherent visualizations to convey the physical and/or conceptual organization of the learning	• Graphic organizers • Concept maps • Sketchnotes • Drawings
Enacting	Generating coherent movements to simulate actions or convey physical and/or conceptual relationships	• Gestures • Object manipulation
Explaining	Generating coherent verbal statements to clarify, interpret, or justify a phenomenon or problem	• Explaining to self or self-verbalization • Teaching others • Comparing • Predicting • Elaborative interrogation

Source: Adapted from Fiorella, L. (2023).

Video 6.3
Visualizing
qrs.ly/vyfya5w

Let's examine how these activities can function as scaffolds for verbal reasoning in complex texts.

- **Visualizing.** Each of the visualization activities in Table 6.5 helps students represent their understanding externally by depicting concept knowledge and relationships. For example, concept maps show a relationship between ideas or concepts. This approach is one way

teachers can help students make sense of their reading by isolating and connecting ideas. If our students struggle to map ideas, then we can push them to develop individual representations first before moving into the reasoning aspects. The ability to visualize through maps and drawings facilitates the explanation (Fiorella, 2023). Further, one study found that students who created sketchnotes (visual notes with writing and drawings) from their reading were twice as likely to remember content compared to those who simply used traditional note-taking methods (Fernandes et al., 2018). And, not surprisingly, drawing allows students time to process and make sense of information as they build a foundation for actively connecting concepts to existing schema.

- **Enacting.** Along with physical enactments and gestures to help students make sense of challenging reading, object manipulation or the use of manipulatives can provide students with key elements in a content text that they must organize into coherent models. Word sorts with physical cardstock or with digital manipulation of word lists require students to organize concepts in meaningful ways. Using chunked texts, students can lift the key ideas off the page to begin sorting and explaining how they fit together.

- **Explaining.** Something positive usually happens to our students' level of understanding when we require them to explain a concept to someone else. Talking allows learners to hear what they know, what they've learned from a text, and what is still fuzzy. Provide students challenging texts to read and ask them to explain their understanding to peers or in a short video. This task affords them additional processing opportunities as well as rehearsal of content. And it provides teachers and students a chance to see what is sticking and what's not.

Each of these generative-learning activities furnishes students opportunities to process, rehearse, and make sense of their reading in meaningful forms of expression while making their thinking and understanding concrete. If your goal is to increase your students' verbal reasoning, then providing ways to make their reasoning visible provides you with the evidence you need to refine and enhance their thinking.

Classroom Practice: Activate Dialogue

We'd be remiss if we didn't explicitly call out discussion as a vehicle to build our students' verbal-reasoning skills. As social learners, our students need their own opportunities to think aloud and process new information, which helps them acquire and consolidate the learning. Hattie's analysis of studies on the subject found that in most classrooms, teachers talked 70 to 80 percent of the time, leaving little space for student dialogue (Hattie, 2023). Hearing someone else talk about a subject (e.g., the teacher) does not ensure students will learn it. However, when students talk about (and thus actively process) learning, the ideas are more likely to stick. Therefore, we need to provide structured opportunities for our students to extract key concepts from texts, summarize, paraphrase, and, ultimately, explain their analyses and conclusions. But how do we structure conversations to support reasoning?

Sometimes concepts are the building blocks of verbal reasoning; other times learners use verbal reasoning to make sense of concepts. By asking our students to extrapolate the ideas and facts from texts, using reasons and evidence, we can set the cornerstone for higher-level thinking. Zwiers and Crawford (2011) explain, "Facts become the raw materials for building ideas, solving problems, thinking critically and creatively, communicating, and transferring concepts to novel situations" (p. 9).

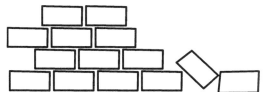

Once students can retrieve concepts, we can prompt them to think deeply about the ideas by engaging text protocols like these:

- *What does the text say? What does the text mean? Why does the text matter?*

- *What do you see? What do you notice? What stands out?*

- *What?* (summarize the text) *So what?* (why does this even matter?) *Now what?* (what can I do with this information?)

When we provide students opportunities to talk, we not only build their verbal skills around academic content but also afford them opportunities to hear how their peers are processing information. Here are some discussion protocols you can include in your classroom as a way to engage all students in conversation, regardless of a student's level of understanding of the text.

- *Five-word summary.* Independently, students choose five words they feel are significant to the text. Students meet with one partner and each shares their five words. Students negotiate to determine which five words they agree upon as most significant. Partners take their newly formed five-word list and share it with another set of partners. Again, the group of four negotiates the top five words. Students independently build a summary from the agreed-upon five-word list.

- *Sentence-phrase-word (also known as text rendering).* Students independently identify the most significant sentence, phrase, and word in the text. Students share in small groups while a scribe records the phrase and the word. Students listen and read the significant phrases and words, and they discuss what each word means in the context of their reading.

- *Discussion roundtable.* Working alone, students take notes on a text. Then, either in a group of four or with three different partners, students take turns speaking, listening, and taking notes about the others' input. Once they have spoken to their group or partners, they write an independent summary about the text based on their own understanding as well as the explanations and notes from their peers (see Figure 6.1).

Figure 6.1 • Discussion Roundtable

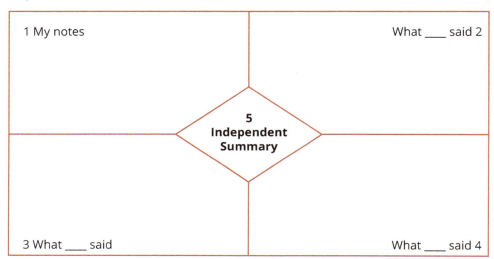

- *Connect-extend-challenge.* Students discuss what concepts in the text they already knew and what those concepts could connect to, what in the text extended their thinking, and what challenged them in terms of concepts they didn't quite understand. Students get the opportunity to verbalize connections and think metacognitively to determine what concepts they didn't grasp.

As your students make sense of their academic reading through discourse, use specific prompts rather than generic ones. For example, saying, "Make an inference about the relationship between these two historical events" is better than saying, "Make an inference." Similarly, saying, "I want you to evaluate the effectiveness of the counterargument in paragraph six" is more specific than saying, "Please evaluate the effectiveness of the author's language." To help our students deepen their verbal reasoning skills, we must use clear, intentional prompts to help build their fluency with understanding how pieces form a whole.

Classroom Practice: Use Distributed and Front-End Scaffolds

Scaffolding is defined as "temporary, assisted learning which tries to create independency in the student" (Malik, 2017, p. 3). We recommend that teachers be wary of reducing the text difficulty levels for texts they teach because a regenerated text may not actually possess the qualities students need to increase their access to it (Lupo et al., 2019). For practice, regenerated texts can be an appropriate scaffold, but texts used for instruction should be appropriately complex. Rather than scaffolding instruction through materials reduction, consider the thinking and verbal reasoning that is required to understand the texts and model those aspects.

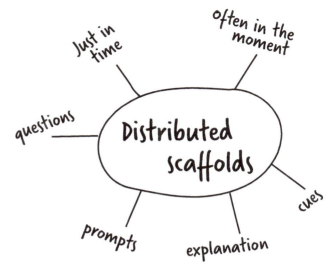

One of the ways to scaffold verbal reasoning is by using *distributed scaffolds*: asking robust questions, providing prompts to activate knowledge, and offering cues to shift students' attention to useful sources (Fisher & Frey, 2010). Distributed scaffolds are sometimes called *just-in-time scaffolds* because they are used in the moment as students falter. Before we continue, let's briefly discuss each of the three types of distributed scaffolds.

Ask Robust Questions

It's essential for students to take on the responsibility of thinking critically so they sharpen their critical-thinking skills as they develop knowledge. For instance, instead of having your students practice making inferences as an isolated practice with a low-level text, you can embed both direct and inferential questions in the margins of a complex text to scaffold the learners' deeper understanding. As you work to scaffold your students' verbal reasoning, you might start by asking robust questions such as the following to identify their understandings, misunderstandings, and partial understandings and then help close gaps in comprehension.

- What information do you already know?
- Can you tell me more about _____?
- Think about what you know already. How would you explain this concept to a third-grade student?
- Are you stuck or are you thinking?

Students often temporarily forget how to utilize information and tools in the face of a new task. So, our questions may make them say, "Oh, I forgot about that!"

As educators, too often we notice only if our students' answers are correct or not. This leads students to play another round of "guess what's in the teacher's head." Instead, we should listen carefully to their answers to gain an understanding of where they are in their learning. Then we can adjust our teaching accordingly. Whether a student gives a right or wrong answer, our goal in questioning is to understand why they have chosen that response. What does the student know or not know that would lead them to that conclusion? This rapid hypothesizing about student thinking is where the art and science of teaching truly intersect.

Provide Prompts as Needed

Just as educators can ask robust questions to check for understanding, we can use prompts as the cognitive nudge our learners sometimes need to foster new thinking. The goal of prompts is to get our students to do the thinking required. Prompts, which often generate "aha! moments," encourage students to consider what they are seeing or might not be seeing in a text. Using prompts, we can encourage our students to draw upon their background knowledge or their understanding of rules or procedures they have been previously taught. Specifically, teachers can prompt learners to do the following:

- Retrieve background knowledge that, at first, is temporarily unavailable (e.g., "What were we learning about yesterday? Can you use that information to help you understand what this writer is saying?")

- Consider their thinking and reflect on their decisions about where they need to go next (e.g., "Your goal this morning was to finish the summary of this article. What do you need to do next to make that happen?")

As another approach, teachers can use sentence stems to activate students' comprehension by prompting them to use their verbal-reasoning skills. Consider the following examples of sentence stems:

- The author's purpose is ____ because ____.

- Tributaries and rivers are similar because ____.

- Kinetic energy is different from potential energy because ____.

- Allies would argue that ____ because ____. The Axis powers believed ____ because ____.

- Patterns I see in the data are ____.

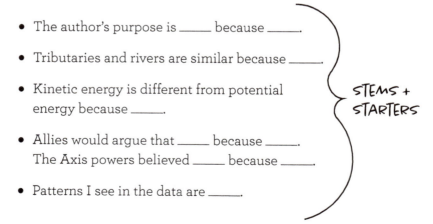

STEMS + STARTERS

Specifically, these prompts can help students consider the relationships between pertinent information or key concepts.

CHAPTER 6 • Verbal Reasoning

Use Cues to Shift Attention to Meaningful Information Sources

Cues are more overt prompts you can use when your students need to shift their attention to a useful source of information. An example is telling students, "Take a look again at the diagram on page seventy-two, and then think about my question again." Like a billiard cue, the classroom cue sets a string of events in motion; they're designed to provide just the right reminder or breakthrough for students to make connections.

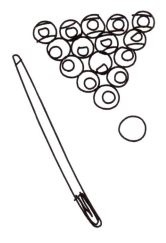

Cues are effective because they shift learners' attention from less salient pieces of information to more relevant ones. Other examples of cues include the following:

- Referencing an anchor chart
- Asking students to reread a section of the text that contains the information they need
- Pointing to an image, graph, or diagram in the text
- Gesturing or using kinesthetic movements to help students link concepts
- Asking learners to revisit a model, template, or frame that will deepen the learning

There are also *front-end scaffolds*, which teachers can put in place prior to the learning. Whereas distributed scaffolds are "just in time," front-end scaffolds are "just in case" (Frey et al., 2023). Students benefit from clear learning intentions and success criteria, which serve not only to prime students' future learning but also to encourage the kind of metacognitive thinking that comes from self-assessing (Fisher et al., 2024). For example, in advance of reading, you can chunk a text to break it up into meaningful sections. Have students read the first text section then ask them to write or say something about it. Once they've read and discussed each section, prompt students to begin synthesizing ideas from across the text.

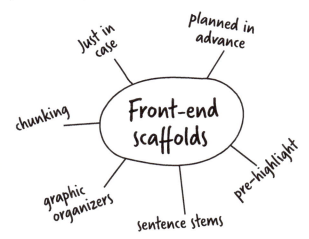

By prehighlighting important information in a text, we can help readers cue their attention to the most critical aspects. Learners still read all of the text, but the key pieces we have already highlighted function as a scaffold for them. By calling out important concepts, we can help our students synthesize and manipulate ideas and see how they fit together.

When teachers combine the use of front-end and distributed scaffolds in the classroom, it can reduce the need to rely on easier texts that are below grade level. Use these scaffolds to foster your students' verbal reasoning, knowledge-building, and metacognitive awareness.

Video 6.4
Tag the Text
qrs.ly/6dfya5x

Voices From the Field

U.S. history teacher Anna Salazar uses success criteria framed as "I can" statements, chunked texts, scaffolded questions, and student dialogue to help her students process ideas individually and synthesize those ideas to draw deeper, more well-informed conclusions. In her classroom she sets up learning stations for small group tasks that students rotate through during the period. Students move from poster to poster, reading, analyzing, and synthesizing information. Figure 6.2 shows an example of one station.

Figure 6.2 • Learning Station in U.S. History

Political and Cultural Change 1: First Red Scare

SC #2: I can use documents to analyze the causes and effects of Roaring 20's economic, political and cultural changes.

"There has come about a general realization of the fact that the races of men who have been coming to us in recent years are wholly dissimilar to the native-born Americans; that they are untrained in self-government—a faculty that it has taken the Northwestern Europeans many centuries to acquire. America was beginning also to grow weak under the irritation of her 'foreign colonies'—those groups of aliens, either in city slums or in country districts, who speak a foreign language and live a foreign life, and who want neither to learn our common speech nor to share our common life. From all this has grown the conviction that it was best for America that our incoming immigrants should hereafter be of the same races as those of us who are already here."

Question 1: What does he believe about the immigrants coming over to America?

Question 2: Where does he want immigrants from?

Credit: Anna Salazar Moss

Through the chunking of texts from historical documents and the combination of right-there and inferential questions, students in Ms. Salazar's class begin to form opinions about the causes and effects of political, economic, and cultural changes during the Roaring '20s. As students move from station to station, Ms. Salazar monitors their progress by checking for student conceptions and misconceptions, scaffolding or extending the questions to help learners move from reading isolated chunks of knowledge to building relationships between them and learning to apply the knowledge in other contexts.

Tenth-grade English teacher Dr. Elena Brittain utilizes scaffolded questions in the margins of digital texts to cue students to focus on what information they should pay particular attention to. This practice helps reduce students' cognitive load by directing their attention to significant chunks of information that allow them to read, analyze, interpret, and derive meaning—all essential for verbal reasoning to occur. Figure 6.3 includes an example from the short story "The Masque of the Red Death" by Edgar Allan Poe; this example shows the addition of Dr. Brittain's cues in the margins of the complex text.

Video 6.5
Scaffolds
qrs.ly/2jg2a8d

Figure 6.3 • Embedded Questions in a Text to Prompt Metacognitive Thinking

decorations of the chamber into which it opened. That at the eastern extremity was hung, for example, in blue—and vividly blue were its windows. The second chamber was purple in its ornaments and tapestries, and here the panes were purple. The third was green throughout, and so were the casements[11]. The fourth was furnished and lighted with orange—the fifth with white—the sixth with violet. The seventh apartment was closely shrouded in black velvet tapestries that hung all over the ceiling and down the walls, falling in heavy folds upon a carpet of the same material and hue. But in this chamber only, the color of the windows failed to correspond with the decorations. The panes here were scarlet—a deep blood color. Now in no one of the seven apartments was there any lamp or candelabrum, amid the profusion of golden ornaments that lay scattered to and fro or depended from the roof. There was no light of any kind emanating from lamp or candle within the suite of chambers. But in the corridors that followed the suite, there stood, opposite to each window, a heavy tripod, bearing a brazier[12] of fire that protected its rays through the tinted glass and so glaringly illumined the

Comment [kb9]: What color is the eastern-most chamber?

Comment [kb10]: What color is the last, western-most room?

What connotations do those colors typically convey?

Why do you think narrator explains the color of every room?

What is the intended effect of the seventh room?

Take Charge: Conclusion and Reflective Questions

This chapter has focused on the crucial role of verbal reasoning, knowledge, and metacognition in reading comprehension. Verbal reasoning in reading refers to the cognitive process of interpreting, analyzing, and deriving meaning from textual content through the manipulation and understanding of language. This includes understanding figurative language and drawing conclusions. Again, we caution against making the content more accessible by reducing the reading level of the text because many of the key opportunities for your students to apply verbal reasoning are absent in easier text. Instead, you can use distributed scaffolds, such as questions, prompts, and cues, to support students' verbal reasoning. Supporting our learners' ability to practice metacognition—which occurs when students reflect on their own thinking—involves planning for learning, monitoring the learning process, and reflecting on the learning process. When we foster metacognition and verbal-reasoning skills, students begin to see reading as a conscious act where they can employ different strategies as needed to comprehend the material.

- Verbal reasoning is a strong predictor of academic achievement, and it grows in its importance as students advance from elementary to secondary school (Tighe & Schatschneider, 2014b). What types of

verbal reasoning—following complex instructions, drawing conclusions, synthesizing information, evaluating for bias, and making inferences—are necessary in your content?

- Direction maintenance helps students attend to relevant information in a task. How can you utilize preplanned questions, prompts, or cues to help draw students' attention to the relevant ideas in a text?

- Automaticity affords learners the opportunity to direct their mental efforts toward solving new tasks with novel information while relying on their thinking habits to do so. What strategies work best in your content to support readers in their development of reasoning?

- How can you utilize embedded text questions, prehighlighting, or chunking to help students think deeply about written and spoken language?

- When students don't read or comprehend well at the secondary level, teachers need to employ all components of scaffolding. When you think about your students who struggle to read, how can you employ strong support to control elements of a task that are beyond the students' current reading ability so the learners still have access to grade-appropriate thinking?

CHAPTER 7

Intervention

Supporting Readers to Develop Automaticity in Word Recognition

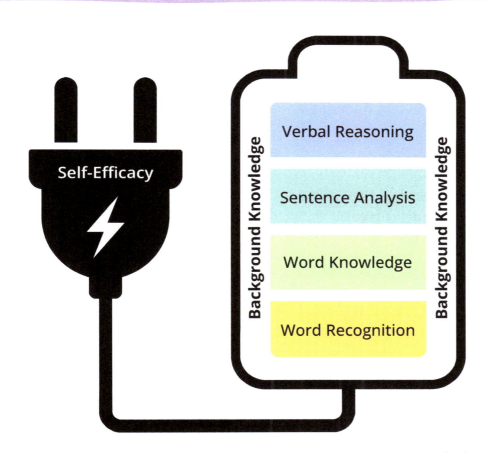

We have established how to put into practice the research on what works for improving the reading skills of students within the context of the classroom, but how can we help students who need the extra support that extends beyond daily instruction? The components of the battery framework are still

present in this chapter but require more intensive support that exceeds the daily demands of quality core instruction.

Students need foundational skills to be successful readers, and there is no expiration date on when these skills can be taught. There is no age limit on learning to read. Students who have previously been unsuccessful in learning to decode arrive with assets that are already there and talents that are waiting to be unveiled. We refer to these students as *aspiring* readers to signify that although they have previously struggled with reading, they are going to receive the support they need to become proficient readers.

With that in mind, as we work with adolescents who still need to acquire basic reading skills, we must be sensitive to the fact that they also may be struggling with a sense of shame. Students who have experienced difficulties learning to read in the past may not feel in control of their ability to learn new skills now. First we must demonstrate our trustworthiness, competence, enthusiasm, and responsiveness to their needs, a concept called *teacher credibility* (Fisher & Frey, 2019). Among the hundreds of influences on student learning, teacher credibility is among the most powerful, with an effect size of 1.09 (Hattie, 2023). Then, as students acquire new skills, we must regularly show them the results of their efforts and assure them that they do have the ability to take on this challenge and that they can self-monitor and problem-solve when reading. These factors foster a growing sense of self-efficacy, which is central to reading attitude and motivation.

Jang and Ryoo's (2019) study of nearly six hundred middle school students examined the interactions between attitude toward reading, reading proficiency, and the medium (print or digital). Although we would like to believe that recreational digital-reading mediums (e.g., text messaging and social media) are motivating for adolescents, this proved not to be the case when it came to those with low reading comprehension. In fact, those students avoided *all* types of reading, whether academic or recreational, whether in print or digitally. Crucially, reading attitudes were strongly predictive of a student's reading proficiency: Those with avoidant attitudes toward reading were the poorest comprehenders. This certainly comes as no surprise; the research on reading volume suggests that the more you read, the more likely your reading proficiency will grow. But Jang and Ryoo (2019) offer a caution to all of us interested in the reading lives of adolescents:

> Cognitive psychology provides only half a solution to the problem of proficiency. Without considering motivation, attitude, and related constructs, we risk focusing on the question of how reading occurs at the expense of asking whether it will

occur and under what conditions. Casting a net broad enough to include both cognitive and affective factors is feasible... to ensure that children will grow up not merely able to read but willing as well. (p. 1789)

Of course, students' skills don't improve simply because we tell them that they are in control or that they can make great things happen. This change happens because teachers systematically design and deliver learning experiences that challenge, yet support, students as they develop. And just as importantly, we attend to their self-efficacy as aspiring readers. This focus ensures that they are motivated by their success and feel courageous enough to take on more challenges.

The purpose of this final chapter is to highlight evidence-based intervention techniques to support the development of word recognition skills for secondary students who fall below the decoding threshold necessary for making gains in reading comprehension. You will recall the discussion on the decoding threshold hypothesis in the chapter on word recognition. The researchers established a decoding threshold for students in grades 5–10 necessary for continued growth in reading comprehension using the Reading Inventory and Scholastic Evaluation (RISE) assessment, which is administered by the Educational Testing Service (Wang et al., 2019). A related research group reported similar findings among college students assigned to remedial developmental reading programs, an institutional marker for adults with reading difficulties (Magliano et al., 2023). Interestingly, the threshold score is virtually the same across grade levels and ages, demonstrating that those who are below the threshold of 235 on the RISE assessment and are in fifth grade or above are unlikely to make gains in reading comprehension in the following years if no intervention occurs.

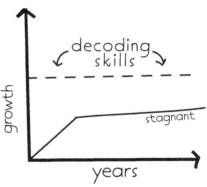

It is also essential to state that not every student who experiences reading difficulties is one who has significant decoding problems. That is why we have framed the premise of this book to highlight the myriad issues that complicate adolescent reading. These components include:

- Self-efficacy in reading
- Background knowledge
- Word recognition
- Sentence analysis
- Verbal reasoning

However, for the smaller number of adolescents who have significant decoding gaps, more specialized intervention is warranted. More personalized small group instruction on decoding and fluency, led by a tutor, can support the needed rise above the decoding threshold. Just as importantly, these word recognition skills need to be linked to reading comprehension through the use of texts.

We use the term *tutor* to describe the adult who leads the lessons. Depending on the school's human resources, the tutor may be a reading specialist, a credentialed teacher assigned to intervention, or a paraprofessional who has been specially trained to deliver this support. It is not a realistic expectation that classroom teachers deliver more intensive decoding interventions inside their content-area classes. However, we believe it is vital that members of school communities possess a working knowledge of what occurs in intervention, what the expectations for monitoring progress are, and how communication loops are developed to ensure that the work interventionists and classroom teachers do is dynamic and amplifies each other's efforts.

Plug Into the Research

A review of ten studies on the long-term effects of reading interventions for adolescents with and without learning disabilities offered good news: Gains made during intervention remained largely in place up to two years after the intervention period (Daniel et al., 2021). During the last two decades, multicomponent reading invention (MCRI) programs have emerged as a sound approach for supporting aspiring adolescent readers. The purpose of a multicomponent approach is to strengthen the dimensions of reading, especially word recognition, word knowledge, and reading comprehension. **A singular focus on isolated word reading, disconnected from meaning and text, is unlikely to yield results** 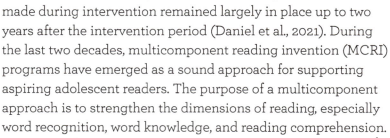 (Scammacca et al., 2007). We offer this perspective somewhat cautiously in light of growing evidence about students who have not yet reached the decoding threshold. Thus, we echo the advice offered by Daniel and colleagues (2022), which is to monitor comprehension frequently. If there is little movement, shift the emphasis of the intervention such that a greater amount of the time is dedicated to word recognition. Once the decoding threshold has been reached, the word recognition component of the lessons can be decreased somewhat to allow for more time on word knowledge and verbal reasoning.

Two characteristics of reading interventions can cause considerable consternation. The first is time and the second is group size. Regarding time, which is always a challenge at the secondary level, the evidence on double-dosing English classes for students who lack basic reading skills is not especially promising. As one example, one large urban district instituted a policy in 2003 for ninth-grade students who read below the national average. These students were assigned a second period of support (and gave

up an elective), but results were mixed, yielding positive results for the weakest readers but also creating the unintended consequences of classroom peer ability, an important driver of student learning (Nomi, 2015). Another study found no positive effects at all (Kidron & Lindsay, 2014). The tension is that for some secondary students, elective courses are motivational for attending school (e.g., Ferrer-Caja & Weiss, 2002). As alternatives, some secondary schools with a higher level of reading needs have exercised changes to the schoolwide master schedule, such as employing a WIN ("what I need") period for students to attend intervention or homework assistance.

A second consideration is group size. Again, there are mixed results when it comes to individual intervention versus small group work. While some studies have found that one-on-one tutoring is promising (Baye et al., 2019), others have demonstrated that the effects are negligible and are not predictors of success (Donegan & Wanzek, 2021; Richards-Tutor et al., 2016). Instead, we recommend group sizes of two to five students, given that cost and personnel limitations are quite real. Having said that, students should be grouped with others who have similar instructional needs, not similar test scores.

Increase Your Battery Life

The following list identifies the nuances and details of effective tutoring sessions. We will then explore these components in more detail throughout the rest of the chapter.

- **Frequency and duration.** It's important to determine the frequency and duration of tutoring sessions. Consider factors like student needs, the need for spaced practice, and scheduling constraints.

- **Identification of students.** It's also essential to establish criteria for identifying students who require reading support. Identify the assessments used to screen for reading difficulties and the scores that indicate extra support is needed.

- **Content and instruction.** Another important step is to define the subjects or topics to be covered. Identify the scope and sequence of reading skills and the specific starting point for each student. Teachers must also decide on research-based structured lessons that address the identified needs (e.g., phonological awareness, phonics, fluency). Include direct instruction, guided practice, interactive activities, feedback, and student application of skill with a connected text to enhance the learning experience.

- **Progress monitoring.** It's also key to establish a system to closely monitor the progress of students receiving tutoring as related to the scope and sequence. Use regular checks for understanding, feedback from students, and master assessments to gauge effectiveness of the intervention. Then make necessary adjustments.

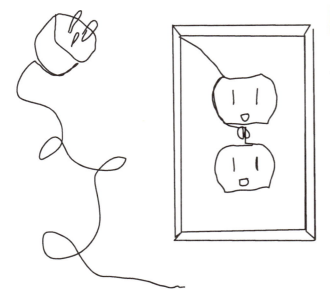

Power Up Classroom Practice

Through this section we will help you identify the answers to the *who, what, when, where,* and *how* of creating an intervention plan or program to support secondary learners with unfinished learning in reading.

Classroom Practice: Identification of Students Who Will Benefit From Tutoring

Let's start with the *who*. Screening tools can help identify students who require individualized tutoring or small group support. Universal screeners are assessments given to all students in a school or district and can be used to determine which students may have reading difficulties.

Schools and teachers can utilize various methods to recognize aspiring readers, including these:

- The previous year's summative/formative assessments
- Norm-referenced assessments
- Universally administered reading comprehension tests

Examples of common universal screening assessments you might already be using include i-Ready Reading, Standardized Test for the Assessment of Reading (STAR), or Measures of Academic Progress (MAP). A district or school must determine what the threshold is on these assessments for students to be considered for intervention.

Video 7.1 Reading Assessment qrs.ly/j3fya5z

Once students have been identified as candidates for further support beyond the classroom setting, educators determine the purpose of the tutoring sessions. To help teachers narrow down what support these learners need, the students undergo further diagnostic evaluation to provide more information about their specific needs and strengths. An example of an assessment that can help to pinpoint what the student already knows and where they need support can be found in Table 7.1. We developed this assessment for use at the high school where we work. It is based on typical items used for early literacy screenings. Table 7.2 contains definitions for the terms used on the assessment.

CHAPTER 7 • Intervention   147

Table 7.1 • Foundational Reading Skills Assessment

ALPHABETICS SKILLS AND KNOWLEDGE OF LETTER AND VOWEL SOUNDS		EXAMPLES FROM THE ASSESSMENT
Letter names (uppercase)	_____/26	*G, R, T*
Letter names (lowercase)	_____/26	*g, r, t*
Consonant sounds	_____/21	*g, r, t*
Short vowel sounds	_____/5	*a, i, u, o, e*
Long vowel sounds	_____/5	*e, a, u, i, o*
Reading and decoding skills		
CVC words	_____/15	*dig, web, lip, rod, jam, cup*
Short vowels and blends	_____/15	*flop, skip, spat, drip, clap, snob, plan, grab*
Short vowels and digraphs	_____/15	*rich, path, chop, ship, mesh, thin*
Final *e*	_____/15	*pine, lake, vote, cube, theme, snake, prize*
Long vowels	_____/15	*spray, soak, flow, bright, honey, sleet, treat*
R-controlled vowels	_____/15	*birth, yarn, mark, churn, firm, herd, blur, fern, perch, torn, stork*
Other variant vowels and diphthongs	_____/15	*mouth, pair, coy, coin, cloud, pause, pull, soup, foot*
Low frequency vowel and consonant spellings	_____/15	*knit, gnaw, crumb, knot, cent, wrote, cell, fence, cave, lamb, stage, germ*
Multisyllabic words (two syllables)	_____/15	*rodent, conflict, upscale, untrain, grumble*
Multisyllabic words (three syllables)	_____/15	*character, fortunate, disagree, dramatic, refugee*

Table 7.2 • Reference List of Assessment Terms

Vowels	Vowels are speech sounds that when produced the airflow of the sound is not restricted by teeth, lips, or tongue. The written representation of vowels are *a, e, i, o, u* and often *y*. For example, in the word *gym*, the *y* serves as a vowel and is pronounced the same as the short *i* sound.
Short vowels	Short vowel sounds are vowel sounds usually represented by vowels: *a, e, i, o,* or *u*; they are pronounced more briefly, like in *apple, bet, hit, soft,* and *up*.
Long vowels	Long vowel sounds occur when a vowel says its name, like in *baby, meet, pie, go,* or *use*.
Consonant sounds	Consonant sounds are sounds produced by consonants. For example, in the word *happy*, we hear two consonant sounds, *h* and *p*. When a word begins with the letter *y*, that indicates it is serving as a consonant, such as in *yellow, yes,* and *yonder*.
CVC words	CVC stands for consonant-vowel-consonant. Words like *cat, bat, hit, get,* and *cup* all follow the CVC pattern.
Blends	Blends occur when consonants are together in a word and each consonant is pronounced individually. For example, in the word *grand*, there are two blends, *gr* and *nd*. When we say the word, we hear *g-r-a-n-d*.
Digraphs	Digraphs are a sequence of two letters that produce only one sound, like in *gnat, chart, dish,* or *what*.
Final *e*	For the purposes of this reading sequence, the final *e* is the *e* at the end of a word that is often silent; sometimes it makes the vowel say its name in words like *game, home, mute,* and *time*. At other times, the *e* is silent but the vowel before it does not say its name, like in *gone* or *lose*.
Diphthongs	Diphthongs are two vowels that are combined in one syllable and the first vowel sound glides into the next vowel sound. It is helpful to remember that *di* in *diphthong* is a Greek word part meaning "two," as in "two sounds." For example, slowly pronounce the word *coin*. You will notice the change in sound as you move from one vowel to the next.
***R*-controlled**	*R*-controlled vowels are vowels that change their pronunciation based on the presence of an *r*. For example, in the word *fork*, the *o* is not short or long; it makes a different sound based on the *r*. It's the same for *absorbent, circuitry, herd,* and *parallel*.
Multisyllabic words	Multisyllabic words contain more than one syllable. Often these are the words secondary students struggle to break apart and read. Understanding where to break multisyllabic words into syllables or meaningful parts is an important skill to develop. For example, we'd break *morphology* into syllables morph/o/log/y, or into its parts with *morph* (meaning form or shape) and *ology* meaning the study of something. Words like *banana* have no word parts in which to extract meaning (ba/na/na).

Classroom Practice: Frequency and Duration of Tutoring Sessions

Establishing the appropriate duration and frequency of tutoring sessions is crucial for providing effective learning support. Research studies offer valuable insights into this aspect of reading intervention. For example, one meta-analysis on effective secondary reading intervention programs identified one successful MCRI that was held for thirty-five minutes once a week and was led by specially trained paraprofessionals (Baye et al., 2019). Additionally, research involving 215 young adolescents (fifth to eighth grade) revealed that struggling readers benefited from small group instruction lasting thirty minutes, conducted either once or twice a week (Reynolds & Goodwin, 2016). This study focused on scaffolding techniques and found that motivational strategies such as gamifying practice and using timed competitions to enhance learning led to student success in comprehending increasingly complex texts. Gamifying practice refers to integrating game elements, such as students being challenged to beat a previous high score. These game elements can be brought into a nongame context like tutoring to increase engagement and motivation. We will come back to this idea when we discuss the content of these sessions.

It is important to note that the thirty-minute intervention implemented in this study occurred in addition to students' regular course work. This approach ensures that students receive specialized support in addition to the core instruction on grade-level standards. Other studies of middle school students suggest shorter intervention sessions of ten to twenty minutes focused on one skill—multisyllabic decoding or fluency—have proven to be effective (Diliberto et al., 2009; Wexler et al., 2008). Our goal is to ensure enough individualized support for students to receive explicit instruction and guided practice without compromising their participation in regular classes or other social and academic opportunities. This necessitates educators to be highly strategic with their tutoring time to effectively deliver instruction. Diagnostic tools such as the Foundational Reading Skills Assessment are informative so the time within these tutoring sessions is maximized to target the specific skills needed. Consider the sample student tutoring schedules in Table 7.3.

Table 7.3 • Sample Schedules for Intervention

	TUESDAY	**THURSDAY**
WIN ("what I need") period	Thirty minutes (12:30pm–1:00pm)	Thirty minutes (12:30pm–1:00pm)

	MONDAY	**WEDNESDAY**	**FRIDAY**
Before school schedule	Twenty minutes before school starts (8:10am–8:30am)	Twenty minutes before school starts (8:10am–8:30am)	Twenty minutes before school starts (8:10am–8:30am)

	MONDAY	**WEDNESDAY**	**THURSDAY**
After school schedule	Twenty minutes immediately after school (3:10pm–3:30pm)	Twenty minutes immediately after school (3:10pm–3:30pm)	Twenty minutes immediately after school (3:10pm–3:30pm)

Classroom Practice: Content and Instruction of the Tutoring Sessions

An MCRI moves students from word reading to connected text. A panel of reading researchers, led by Sharon Vaughn, reviewed studies for the What Works Clearinghouse, an initiative of the U.S. Department of Education's Institute of Education Sciences. Their review of interventions for older students produced four recommendations (Vaughn et al., 2022, p. 3):

1. Build students' decoding skills so they can read complex multisyllabic words.

2. Provide purposeful fluency-building activities to help students read effortlessly.

3. Routinely use a set of comprehension-building practices to help students make sense of the text.

4. Provide students with opportunities to practice making sense of stretch text (i.e., challenging text) that will expose them to complex ideas and information.

The variance is in how time is distributed across MCRI lessons. For students who have not yet attained the decoding threshold, comparatively more time should be spent on word recognition. For those who have cleared the decoding threshold, the entry point may be at the level of decoding multisyllabic words.

As discussed earlier, our assessment pinpoints the areas of support for word recognition that serve as the focus of tutoring sessions. We will explore

Video 7.2 Scope and Sequence qrs.ly/5sfya62

common needs and what instruction can look like during the tutoring sessions, including teaching students how to decode, starting with single-syllable words, reading fluency, and comprehension. Within these areas of focus, these tutoring sessions should have routines and structures in place that maximize the efficiency of each session. Therefore, we will look at effective tutoring as requiring both systematic and explicit instruction, as defined here:

- *Systematic instruction* follows an evidence-based scope and sequence.
- *Explicit instruction* requires that teachers intentionally design and there is direct instruction, explanation, and modeling.

Classroom Practice: Systematic Instruction in Word Recognition

Before we go into more detail about the tutoring structure, let's define what we mean by phoneme-grapheme correspondences. *Graphemes* are the written symbols of spoken language—the letters or groups of letters that represent the sounds of a language. There can be between one and four graphemes that represent a single sound. *Phonemes* are the sounds made by those graphemes, and sometimes one phoneme can be represented by more than one grapheme. In other words, there is more than one way to write a sound. For example, the /f/ phoneme can be represented as the letter *f*, like in *farm*, or the letters *ph*, like in *phone*. Therefore, phoneme-grapheme correspondences are the match between a sound and the letter or letters represented by that sound. Table 7.4

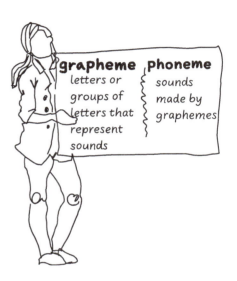

Table 7.4 • Examples of Phoneme-Grapheme Correspondences

PHONEME (SOUND)	MOST COMMON GRAPHEME THAT REPRESENTS THE PHONEME	OTHER GRAPHEMES THAT REPRESENT THE PHONEME
consonant /d/	*d* as in *dig*	*dd* as in *add* *ed* as in *cleaned*
consonant /j/	*j* as in *jump*	*ge* as in *barge* *g* as in *giant* *_dge* as in *nudge*
long vowel /ā/	*ai* as in *strain*	*a* as in *acorn* *a_e* as in *bake* *ei* as in *veil* *eigh* as in *eight* *aight* as in *straight* *ey* as in *they* *ay* as in *stray*

provides examples of these correspondences. There are forty-four different phonemes in the English language, and these sounds are combined to form words. Explicit and systematic instruction means that we determine what the student's entry point into this work is, based on data, and then directly teach how the sounds of the language are connected into print.

This direct instruction is followed by guided practice, leading students toward independent application of skills. The instructional design must be purposeful, aligning with the overarching goal of enhancing students' phonics skills. Understanding the sequential development of these skills is crucial for teaching students to decode effectively. This sequence serves as an instructional path. However, when it comes to older aspiring readers, it is likely that they have a scattered profile when it comes to these skills, with gaps along the sequence. Therefore, students may progress somewhat differently across this continuum. While different curricula may slightly vary in their identified scope and sequence, they are organized by increasing levels of difficulty. For example, students are first taught short vowels and consonants so they can be taught to blend these sounds together to form VC (vowel-consonant) words like *on, in,* and *at,* as well as CVC (consonant-vowel-consonant) words such as *dig, mop,* and *hat.* The scope and sequence make up the instructional roadmap and allow for accurate progress monitoring. Figure 7.1 includes an example of a scope and sequence.

Video 7.3
Explicit Instruction
qrs.ly/pwfya64

Classroom Practice: Explicit Instruction in Word Recognition

It is important to note that not all aspiring readers need this level of instruction. The use of diagnostic assessments is crucial for determining where the entry point should be for a multicomponent reading intervention. Once we understand where our work is situated within the sequence of instruction, educators can plan for the explicit instruction in each session. Let's look at a sample lesson for a student who does not possess fundamental knowledge of early phonics development. The lesson centers on the first recommendation forwarded by Vaughn and colleagues (2022), which is to build phonics skills so students will be able to accurately decode multisyllabic words. We will first situate the lesson within the sequence being used in Table 7.5. In this sequence, the student has mastered the skills in yellow.

So, the next lesson is on the /j/ sound that can be written by the letter *j*, like in the word *jelly*, or the cluster of letters *-dge*, like in the word *judge*. Table 7.6 highlights a sample lesson introducing the /j/ sound, which can be written with the following graphemes: *j* and *-dge*. The lesson also includes practice of sound-letter correspondences that have already been taught.

CHAPTER 7 • Intervention

Figure 7.1 • Sample Progression of Phonics Skills

								Multisyllabic words (syllable types)
							Multisyllabic words (prefix/ suffix)	
						r-controlled vowels, variants, dipthongs		
					Long vowels			
				Final *e*				
			Short vowels and digraphs					
		Short vowels and blends						
	Short vowels and consonants							
ABCs								

Source: Fisher, D., Frey, N. & Lapp, D. (2023).

Table 7.5 • Scope and Sequence With Short Vowels, Consonants, Digraphs, Blends, and Final-*e* Words

m	a	s	t	p	f	i	n	o	d	c	u	g	b	e	s	k, ck	h	r	l
w	j, -dge	y	x	qu	v	z	ff, ll, ss, zz	sh	th	ch	wh	_ng	_nk	blends	a_e	i_e	o_e	e_e	u_e

Table 7.6 • Sample Foundational Skills Lesson Plan

EXAMPLE SESSION STRUCTURE	EXAMPLE LESSON WITH SAMPLE SCRIPT FOR THE TEACHER
1. *Phonemic awareness* This portion of the lesson involves the students being able to manipulate the sounds of the language using one of these skills: - Phoneme isolation - Blending sounds - Segmenting sounds - Addition - Deletion In this lesson, the student is orally blending sounds.	"First, we will practice blending sounds together to make words. I will say three sounds, and you blend the sounds together to make a word. Watch my finger as I point and say each sound." **Teacher:** "/m/ /e/ /n/" **Student:** "*Men.*" Repeat the process with the following words: *dodge, jam, tip, cub, fudge*
2. *Focus lesson and guided instruction: phonics* - Introduce the new phoneme-grapheme correspondences. - Show visual support.	"Today we are learning two ways to write the sound /j/. The sound /j/ is written with the letter *j*, like in *jump*, and the sound /j/ is also written *dge*." **Teacher:** "Okay, now your turn. What sound does *dge* make?" **Student:** "/j/." **Teacher:** "What sound does this letter make [pointing to letter *j*]?" **Student:** "/j/."
3. *Review of phonemes/graphemes that have been introduced in previous lessons with the new ones introduced in this lesson* - Student practices new sounds and applies sounds to reading words with support and feedback from the teacher.	"It is important for us to practice the new sounds and the sounds we have already learned so they become automatic for us and we get faster and remember each one." Teacher shows index cards with a grapheme on each card or a table of all the phoneme-grapheme correspondences that have been taught as the student says the sound of each one. Example: <table><tr><td>*p*</td><td>*d*</td><td>*e*</td><td>*r*</td></tr><tr><td>*f*</td><td>*j*</td><td>*s*</td><td>*l*</td></tr><tr><td>*i*</td><td>*u*</td><td>*k*</td><td>*_dge*</td></tr><tr><td>*n*</td><td>*g*</td><td>*o*</td><td>*b*</td></tr><tr><td>*h*</td><td>*_ck*</td><td>*c*</td><td>*w*</td></tr><tr><td>*m*</td><td>*a*</td><td>*t*</td><td>*k*</td></tr></table> The teacher provides feedback.

EXAMPLE SESSION STRUCTURE	EXAMPLE LESSON WITH SAMPLE SCRIPT FOR THE TEACHER
4. *Application of skills* - Student applies their knowledge of phoneme-grapheme relationships to read words.	"Now you will read words. Remember that you know all of the sounds in the words I am going to show you. If you get stuck, you can tap and say each sound before you blend them together." **Teacher:** "Read these words that have the sounds we have practiced: *judge, duck, nudge, gum, nod, rim, badge, pad, edge.*" Teacher provides feedback.
5. *Focus lesson and guided instruction: high-frequency words* - Teacher introduces a word and the student repeats the word, spells out the letters of the word, and reads the word again. - Teacher and student discuss what makes each high-frequency word a little tricky.	"Now we are going to work on our high-frequency words. Remember these are words that show up a lot in the books that all students and adults read every day." Introduce each work by reading the word to the student then having the student read, spell, and reread the word. Discuss why this word might be difficult to read or spell. 1. *Have*: Explain that this word may be difficult because the letters *h*, *a*, and *v* all seem to follow the rules we have learned so far, but the *e* doesn't make a short *e* sound, like it has been practiced. Explain that the letter *e* has lots of roles in written language and one job it has is to protect words from ending in *v* or *f*. In this word, it doesn't make a sound, or change the sound of any letters, but it still plays an important role in ensuring the word *have* doesn't end in the letter *v*. 2. *Does*: The teacher can explain why this word is difficult for some students or can ask the student, "Why is this a tricky word for many readers?" A possible response would be, "The first sound matches the letter *d*, and the last sound matches the letter *s*, but the middle sound is /u/ although the letter is not *u*."
6. *Spiral review of high-frequency words* - Student is presented with high-frequency words that have been explicitly taught in step five. - The list includes the high-frequency words introduced in this lesson. Notice that *have* and *does* are included in this review.	Student reads previously introduced high-frequency words in a randomized order. <table><tr><td>about</td><td>from</td><td>are</td><td>have</td></tr><tr><td>be</td><td>he</td><td>my</td><td>make</td></tr><tr><td>there</td><td>to</td><td>or</td><td>for</td></tr><tr><td>people</td><td>would</td><td>said</td><td>her</td></tr><tr><td>the</td><td>many</td><td>go</td><td>first</td></tr><tr><td>all</td><td>ball</td><td>fall</td><td>call</td></tr><tr><td>is</td><td>then</td><td>play</td><td></td></tr></table>

(Continued)

(Continued)

EXAMPLE SESSION STRUCTURE	EXAMPLE LESSON WITH SAMPLE SCRIPT FOR THE TEACHER
7. *Guided instruction of application through encoding (spelling)* - Student repeats words that are orally dictated to them. - Student segments the sounds in a word in preparation for spelling the word. - Notice that all words the student is being asked to spell are either high-frequency words that were explicitly taught or include only consonant and vowel sounds that have been explicitly taught.	"Now it is time for you to take what you have learned and apply that to your spelling. You will spell five words and one sentence. Remember that you know all of these sounds because we have practiced them all." **Teacher:** "The fish has a fin. Say *fin*." **Student:** "Fin." **Teacher:** "Say the sounds you hear in the word *fin*." **Student:** "/f/i/n/" **Teacher:** "Now, spell the word." The student writes the word on paper or a whiteboard. Continue with this routine using the following words: *judge, cub, edge, tap*. "It's time for your sentence. Repeat this sentence: *The cup is on the edge.* Write a line for every word in that sentence then write your sentence, including a capital letter and correct punctuation."
8. *Reading a connected text* - Student reads the text aloud. The text should be read more than once. Fluency practice can include rereading, reading in phrases, practice with intonation and expression, exploring the meaning of punctuation, etc.	My Pet Rob and I went to the pet shop. That is when I got Doc. Is Doc a rat? No. Is Doc a crab? No. Doc is my pet dog. Doc is a ball of fun. He has soft, tan fur. This dog has a black spot on his leg. Doc runs in the sun. He sits on my lap for a nap. My plan was to play with Doc. I said, "Doc, play with me. We can play dodge-ball." Doc sat and did not play. I said, "Doc, get this rag." Doc sat and did not play. I said, "Get the ball. It is on the edge of the bed." Doc got the ball, then I gave Doc a snack. I am glad I have Doc as a pet.

Video 7.4 Systematic Instruction qrs.ly/j5fya68

Although this is only one example of a structured phonics lesson, it includes several important attributes. The focus of the lesson is the direct and explicit instruction of the newly introduced phonics concept. Following this instruction, students engage in practice and apply and consolidate their understanding. Additionally, the incorporation of spiral review, or the opportunity to practice and reinforce skills within the lesson, draws upon the research on deliberate practice (Willingham, 2021). This strategic integration ensures reinforcement of previously learned concepts, enhancing the students' mastery over time. The final component of the lesson was for the student to read a connected text. This element is crucial and cannot be skipped because students need to spend time decoding words across sentences, and not just in isolation. This text was specifically designed to be decodable, meaning that the passage contains words and spelling patterns that have already been specifically taught in previous lessons. This is the place where students get to apply what they have learned and build their fluency. We will discuss fluency in more detail in the next section.

The practice and application of learning falls under the category of guided instruction. Teachers actively support students by offering prompts and cues in response to student needs. Teachers should not provide answers but rather guide the students' thought process. During guided practice, students will make mistakes, and teachers need to be prepared to respond in a manner that doesn't remove the cognitive load from students. Simply providing the correct answer for students doesn't help the educator understand why the error was made or help the student (Fisher et al., 2010). Instead, teachers should provide prompts to engage metacognition or cues to direct a student's attention to the error. After beginning with prompts, educators then transition to cues if the initial prompt proves unsuccessful. Prompts are used initially to spark prior knowledge; cues are more overt and shift the student's attention to salient information they may have overlooked. Table 7.7 provides examples of prompts and cues for some common student mistakes.

Introducing the routines and structure for tutoring might require a couple of lessons, but students quickly adapt and become comfortable with the expectations. They thrive on the success that rapidly builds.

Table 7.7 • Prompts and Cues for Miscues

STUDENT MISCUE	PROMPT	CUE
Student said *bed* instead of *bid*.	Think about the card we use for the short vowel *i*. Remember that the middle vowel can be tricky and we really need to pay attention to the vowel.	Look at the vowel in the word again. The vowel *i* makes the /i/ sound. Try again. [Teacher points to the short *i* picture card.] "Look at the image of the igloo."
Student gets stuck when spelling the word *nudge*.	What strategy can you use before you spell a word?	First break the word *nudge* into its three sounds.
Student reads a sentence disfluently.	Did that sentence sound like speaking? How can you read this sentence using the chunking strategy?	[Teacher draws swoops underneath phrases in the sentences.] "Read the sentence again using these phrase chunks."

Classroom Practice: Fluency

We discussed reading fluency in Chapter 3 with word recognition, but now we revisit this skill with a focus on how to support reading fluency for students receiving small group or individual tutoring on reading foundational skills. Oral reading fluency assessments are a great resource for educators when they begin tutoring students to support their reading skills. These assessments are a particularly useful tool because they are time efficient to administer. Further, they are helpful for monitoring secondary student progress in word recognition interventions (Washburn, 2023).

Improving reading fluency for secondary students is not just about reading faster; it also includes reading with expression and using appropriate phrasing, called prosody. Equally important is that a student's brain is effortlessly decoding words. The surface view of fluency instruction is that students are taught to read faster, but the deeper view is that students are building the decoding skills for reading comprehension (Pikulski & Chard, 2005). When students are not struggling to sound out the word parts, they can pay greater attention to the meaning of the words and how they connect together within the sentences and within the passage. For this reason, fluency-building is the second recommendation for MCRI programs (Vaughn et al., 2022).

Repeated Readings

Repeated readings have been shown to increase the speed and accuracy not only of the passage that students are practicing but also of new reading passages, and they are an effective part of an MCRI program for adolescents (Denton et al., 2008). However, it is important to note that students need to be reading to an adult during these tutoring sessions because it is imperative that the adult provide modeling and corrective feedback (Wexler et al., 2008). Additionally, students can benefit from self-assessment opportunities to listen to a recording of their reading, noting areas for improvement and progress. Consider the rubric in Table 7.8 as a tool for students to use to self-assess and gauge their learning. As noted in the earliest chapters, self-efficacy—the belief that you can achieve your goals—is fueled by evidence that you are indeed making progress toward those goals.

Some students might be motivated to continue practicing their fluency by seeing improvement in their fluency, but others might find repeated readings, well, a little repetitive. In that case, a great alternative is for students to read the same amount of text, but from different passages (Wexler et al., 2008). For example, students could read four different short texts around a similar topic instead of reading one text four times. Either strategy benefits students, for whom having a model for fluent reading and someone who can provide feedback is essential (Wexler et al., 2008). Before we move on, let's explore a few more activities that teachers can integrate into their students' fluency practice.

CHAPTER 7 • Intervention   159

Table 7.8 • Fluency Rubric

THIS IS AN AREA OF "GROWTH" FOR ME.	SUCCESS CRITERIA	THIS IS AN AREA OF "GLOW" FOR ME.
	I can read each word in the text accurately.	
	If needed, I can ask for a word to be pronounced for me so I can read it accurately.	
	I can read at the right speed—not too slow, not too fast.	
	I can read and emphasize parts of sentences to make the text sound more interesting.	
	I can make my voice go up and down in the right places when I read.	
	I can notice when I make a mistake when reading and fix it.	
	I can read groups of words together to make them sound like I am talking.	
	I can notice how my reading improves each time I read the text aloud.	

Phrase Progressions

A key to prosody, which is the "musical quality" of reading fluency, is to understand the phrase boundaries that bind a series of words together in a meaningful way (Worthy & Broaddus, 2001/2002, p. 334). Sentences are comprehended in part as a series of meaningful noun and verb phrases. Use phrase progressions to warm students up to a text before reading the entire passage. The fluency pyramid technique, developed by the Florida Center for Reading Research, breaks a sentence into chunks. Crucially, each phrase should retain meaning on its own.

In preparation for a fluency pyramid activity, the teacher types the initial phrase of the sentence on the first line. On the second line, the teacher types the first and second phrases of the sentence. Each additional line adds one more phrase of the sentence. The final line displays the complete sentence. Each line is uncovered one by one for the student to read.

Video 7.5
Fluency Pyramid
qrs.ly/f1fya6c

Table 7.9 contains two examples of a phrase progressions. The first is for students who are decoding single-syllable words, and it comes from a story about a young man who buys his first truck. In this decodable text, the student has been taught all the phoneme-grapheme correspondences as well as words with irregular patterns. The second example starts a passage about a volcanic eruption.

Table 7.9 • Phrase Progressions

ONE-SYLLABLE WORDS	MULTISYLLABIC WORDS
When I	
When I was sixteen,	The volcano
When I was sixteen, I got	The volcano erupted
When I was sixteen, I got an old,	The volcano erupted with a fury
When I was sixteen, I got an old, scratched,	The volcano erupted with a fury that startled everyone.
When I was sixteen, I got an old, scratched, red truck.	

Roll the Inference

Reading with expression is the bridge to reading comprehension and reflects knowledge of the emotional prosody aligned to the meaning of the sentence. When our vocal rate or intonation changes, we are reflecting our understanding of a concept or idea. This game is an engaging way to get students to experiment with the tone, pacing, and emphasis of their voice. The sentences can be changed based on skills the students are working on, or to connect to work being done in their classrooms. Here is how the game works:

1. The student rolls the die the first time and reads the sentence that corresponds with the number on the die.

2. The student rolls the die a second time and then reads the same sentence with the emotion that corresponds to the number on the die of the second roll:

   - 1 = anxiousness or nervousness.
   - 2 = sad or lonely.
   - 3 = happy or informative.
   - 4 = suspicious.
   - 5 = angry or frustrated.
   - 6 = tired or bored.

The student then makes an inference as to whether they think the author would agree with a particular emotion for the sentence. For example, a small group of eighth-grade students who were reading *The Outsiders* by S. E. Hinton (1967) in their English class played a round of the inference game during their MCRI. Some of the sentences used included the following:

- "I lie to myself all the time. But I never believe me."

- "They grew up on the outside of society. They weren't looking for a fight. They were looking to belong."

- "You get tough like me and you don't get hurt. You look out for yourself and nothin' can touch you."

- "He died violent and young and desperate, just like we all knew he'd die someday."

- "I am a greaser. I am a JD and a hood. I blacken the name of our fair city. I beat up people. I rob gas stations. I am a menace to society. Man do I have fun!"

- "I'd rather have anybody's hate than their pity."

When possible, use sentences that are conceptually connected to the content students are learning in the classroom. This approach provides the opportunity to double-dose knowledge-building even as you are working on foundational reading skills. In addition, it bridges the third and fourth recommendations from the panel on MCRI programs—namely, reading connected texts and introducing stretch text passages that offer a bit more challenge (Vaughn et al., 2022).

Classroom Practice: Morphology and Word Study

In Chapter 4 on word knowledge, we discussed using morphology instruction to support word, sentence, and passage comprehension in the content classroom. But morphology can also be introduced during tutoring sessions when a student is learning to decode. Inflectional endings are morphological parts that usually appear as suffixes at the end of a free morpheme. For example, let's say students have learned how to decode a word like *bed*. The teacher can then explicitly teach how the *-s* at the end of a word sometimes signals that the word is plural. Later, students can be taught that the inflectional ending *-ed*, which can make three different sounds—/t/, /d/, or /id/—can be added to the end of a verb to signal past tense. See Table 7.10 for inflectional endings that carry meaning (convey tense, plurality, possession, or comparison) and that can be explicitly taught after students have learned to connect graphemes and morphemes and are blending them to read words. Notice that at this level, the inflectional endings carry meaning but they do not change the part of speech of the word.

Table 7.10 • Inflectional Endings

INFLECTIONAL ENDING	FREE MORPHEME	NEW WORD WITH INFLECTIONAL MORPHEME	PURPOSE
-s	*truck*	*trucks*	To make plural
-es	*box*	*boxes*	To make a noun plural when the word ends in *ch, sh, ss,* or *x*
-ing	*play*	*playing*	To communicate present tense; that the verb is currently happening
-ed with three different sounds /d/, /t/, or /id/	*walk*	*walked*	To communicate past tense; the verb already happened
-'s	*cat*	*cat's*	To indicate possession (belonging to someone or something)
-s'	*parents*	*parents'*	To indicate possession (belonging to multiple parents)
-er	*fast*	*faster*	To compare two things
-est	*fast*	*fastest*	To compare more than two things
-en	*eat*	*eaten*	To form the past participle tense

Suffix Sorts

Some suffixes are more challenging and can confound students who are learning how they are used as well as how they are spelled. Use suffix sorts to highlight spelling and parts of speech used in each challenging word. Assemble lists of four to six words representing a pair of similar suffixes and print them on index cards. For example, the words *expectancy, occupancy, vacancy,* and *discrepancy* can be sorted in the *-ancy* pile of cards, while

CHAPTER 7 • Intervention

currency, emergency, fluency, and *tendency* can be sorted in the *-ency* word pile. Don't squander the chance to build vocabulary, writing skills, and sentence-level knowledge by discussing the meanings of each word, composing sentences containing the words, and rereading the sentences for further fluency work. Table 7.11 contains a list of confusing noun and adjective suffixes that can trip up aspiring readers.

Table 7.11 • Confusing Suffixes

CONFUSING SUFFIX	EXAMPLE WORDS
-ance and *-ence*	*maintenance* and *absence*
-ancy and *-ency*	*vacancy* and *urgency*
-ant and *-ent*	*brilliant* and *different*
-acy and *-sy*	*legacy* and *courtesy*
-ary, -ory, and *-ery*	*dictionary, laboratory,* and *monastery*
-able and *-ible*	*preferable* and *sensible*
-ion and *-ian*	*impression* and *draconian*
-er, -ar, and *-or*	*customer, scholar,* and *indicator*
-tion and *-sion*	*generalization* and *permission*

Word Sums

Students who are learning how to decode multisyllabic words benefit from seeing how words are built. Word sums are visual representations of meaningful components of words using plus signs (Bowers & Kirby, 2010). For example, the word *redesigning* is represented as *re + de + sign + ing* and is read aloud in parts, including the plus signs. Begin with words that use affixes that do not change the spelling, such as *corruptible* and *separately,* and progress to derivations that do alter the spelling pattern, such as going from *judgment* to *judicial.* Word sums can be arranged using note cards containing various word parts. As students progress to more complex words, they can use a word sum matrix (see Table 7.12 as an example). Words are built across the word matrix from left to right.

Table 7.12 • Word Sum Matrix

de *in* *pre* *re*	*fer*	*ed* *s* *ing*
trans		*able* *al*

Classroom Practice: Passage Reading of Complex Texts

Intervention lessons focused on adolescent reading should include opportunities to read more complex text, which is the fourth recommendation for MCRI programs (Vaughn et al., 2022). Opatz and Kocherhans (2024) studied the impact of integrating complex text in intervention efforts on seventh-grade aspiring readers who participated in a yearlong MCRI program in small groups, led by trained paraprofessionals. The components of the program mirrored those described in this chapter: attention to word recognition, fluency, word study of multisyllabic words, and passage reading of complex texts. The students in the study made significant gains of nearly two years' of grade equivalency, a demonstration of accelerated learning well above the expected one year of growth. These findings align with those reported in our study of an after-school close-reading intervention for middle school students (Fisher & Frey, 2014).

The use of more complex text passages in the MCRI is instructive. This part of the lesson consisted of a short introduction to the topic by the tutor and a preview of challenging vocabulary, which lasted approximately one minute. The tutor then read the text passage aloud while the students chorally read, using an echo reading approach in which a short section of the passage (one or two sentences) is read first by the teacher, then chorally read by the students.

After completing the challenge passage, the small group engaged in discussion of the meaning of the text using text-dependent questions (see Chapter 5 for a review of text-dependent questions). After the discussion, students reread the same passage independently and silently. Once finished, the tutor asked additional text-dependent questions designed to deepen and extend their comprehension.

In sum, a successful MCRI for adolescents needs to include some time with connected text that serves to stretch them a bit. Not only does it allow for the application of word recognition skills, fluency, and word study skills but it also contributes to their background knowledge, which is vital for adolescents who must read and comprehend texts across content areas. The use of more complex texts in this context is a consistent throughline for adolescent MCRI programs (Barth & Elleman, 2017; Denton et al., 2008).

Take Charge: Conclusion and Reflective Questions

If a student hasn't previously learned to decode single-syllable or multisyllabic words, then now is the right time for them to learn. It is never too late to learn to read. Students at any age can receive systematic and explicit instruction to unlock the code to a word reading and of meaning. This chapter advocates for a proactive approach in identifying and supporting students who require foundational reading skills, which are then extended to include vocabulary and text reading. Your ability to reflect on the impact of your teaching, along with systematic progress monitoring of the students' learning, are necessary to determine the effectiveness of the interventions. Educators can create a supportive environment where every student has the opportunity to excel in their reading skills, regardless of their previous challenges.

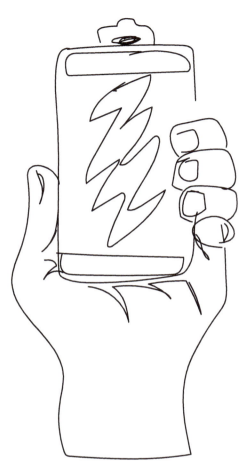

- Word recognition and phonics are not concepts many secondary teachers feel most comfortable teaching, yet many of our students struggle to simply decode. How can you build in intervention time for these readers who cannot yet read well?

- Screening tools are essential for determining which students have unfinished learning in the area of reading. Determine which literacy assessments your school site is already using that can be used as a universal assessment to identify students. What follow-up assessment will you use to pinpoint the students' needs?

- It's not fun to read when you can't do it well, so many students will disengage with reading tasks. Which strategies mentioned in this chapter do you feel confident that, with practice, you could implement effectively to help students who can't read well yet?

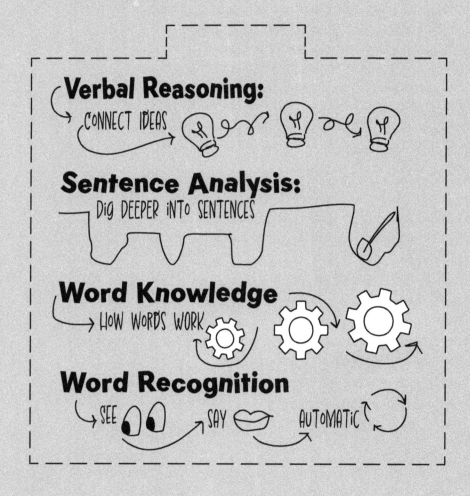

Coda

Teaching foundational skills to older readers is an important aspect of the job that middle and high school teachers do. We are not suggesting that all teachers are teachers of reading, but rather that all teachers can foster students' reading habits and skills. There is a difference here that is noteworthy. Some students require extensive support to develop their reading skills, which is why we included a chapter on intervention in this book. However, most students need to continue the progress they made in elementary school. Failure to continually make progress in reading across grades 6–12 will result in more students who need intervention services. Thus, all teachers need to understand some aspects of the reading process if they are going to be successful.

We have proposed a model for adolescent reading development. Our model acknowledges the powerful role that self-efficacy plays in learning and learning to read well. Utilizing isolated strategy instruction or interventions without attending to self-efficacy will not produce the results that students deserve. Instead, their teachers should recognize the role of self-efficacy and integrate the development of efficacious behaviors in their ongoing interactions with students.

We have also noted the importance of knowledge. Recognizing that there is a threshold of knowledge under which students will struggle with learning and reading is also important for teachers. When teachers develop and activate relevant knowledge, students learn more and also develop stronger reading skills.

Inside the model are four critical aspects for teaching reading. Together with self-efficacy and background knowledge, we argue that these are foundational skills for adolescents. We recognize that these are not the traditional foundational skills discussed for younger readers, but we hopefully have convinced you that they are nonnegotiable in terms of adolescent reading development. Thus, we must consider them foundational, not optional. The skills we recognize as foundational for adolescents are:

- *Word recognition:* learning to recognize increasing numbers of words by sight, having learned how to decode and pronounce the words
- *Word knowledge:* understanding the ways that words work, both in terms of syllables and morphology and in recognizing the meaning, or often multiple meanings, of words

167

- *Sentence analysis:* evaluating syntax and grammar to understand how words are used in connected texts, which can influence the connotations of words and the logical inferences that can be made
- *Verbal reasoning:* applying logic to longer pieces of text that require more detailed analyses, including evaluation and critical thinking

The question is, how do we know if we are developing these skills in our students? Below we provide several questions you can ask yourself or your team to identify areas of strength and potential areas of growth.

- In the area of self-efficacy:
  - Do students know their current level of performance in reading?
  - Do students have goals for their learning that include reading?
  - Are students provided with feedback about their progress in reading?
  - Do teachers make a direct connection between effort and increased performance in reading?
- In the area of knowledge building:
  - Do teachers recognize the critical knowledge needed to understand the text?
  - Do teachers have tools to identify students' knowledge levels, such as anticipation guides, initial assessments, or advance organizers?
  - Do teachers activate relevant background knowledge but spend too many instructional minutes on knowledge that is tangential?
  - Do teachers select text sets that build knowledge as they increase text complexity and difficulty?
- In the area of word recognition:
  - Do teachers recognize the value of teaching students to recognize words at sight?
  - Do teachers have specific content words that they need students to recognize?
  - Do teachers engage students in fluency practice?
  - Do teachers provide a model of fluent reading for students?
- In the area of word knowledge:
  - Is academic vocabulary taught and practiced in every lesson?
  - Do teachers strategically decide between telling students word meanings, analyzing the text for word meanings, and directly teaching words?
  - Do teachers model word-solving using morphology and context clues during reading?

o Are morphological patterns taught and assessed?

o Are syllable patterns taught and assessed?

- In the area of sentence analysis:

    o Do teachers identify specific sentences to dissect with their students?

    o Are specific syntax and grammar patterns identified for instruction?

    o Are students' errors and needs used to design instruction in grammar?

    o Are students taught to read closely?

- In the area of verbal reasoning:

    o How do teachers define verbal reasoning? Do they include the dimensions identified by the Educational Testing Service?

    o Are comprehension strategies explicitly taught?

    o Do students have opportunities to collaborate with others, sharing their reasoning and exploring the reasoning of their peers?

    o Do teachers strategically use scaffolds to support students' learning?

- In the area of intervention:

    o Are students identified for supplemental and intensive intervention based on evidence?

    o Are intervention schedules developed and implemented that ensure that identified students receive the intervention?

    o Is the content of the intervention aligned with the student's needs? For example, if the student is below the decoding threshold, is the focus on decoding?

    o Are students monitored during intervention to ensure that the efforts have the desired impact?

All of these are important considerations if teachers, teams, and schools are going to ensure that students continue their upward trajectory in reading. Reading has always been a critical skill, but more recently it has become one that is on the decline. As noted in the National Endowment for the Arts publication *Reading at Risk* (www.arts.gov/sites/default/files/RaRExec.pdf), people are reading less and less—and not just when considering reading for pleasure. When the adolescents of today enter adulthood, reading and analyzing what they read will be even more critical. A great deal of text is being generated, including the synthetic texts generated by artificial intelligence, that have the potential to inform or mislead readers. Being able to read well will continue to separate those who are successful from those who are not. Nothing less than our students' future is at stake. Teach reading well and your students will reap the benefits.

References

Ahmed, Y., Francis, D. J., York, M., Fletcher, J. M., Barnes, M., & Kulesz, P. (2016). Validation of the direct and inferential mediation (DIME) model of reading comprehension in grades 7 through 12. *Contemporary Educational Psychology, 44*, 68–82. 10.1016/j.cedpsych.2016.02.002

Alexander, P. A., & Fox, E. (2011). Adolescents as readers. In M. L. Kamil, P. D. Pearson, E. B. Moje, & P. P. Afflerbach (Eds.), *Handbook of reading research* (Vol. IV, pp. 157–176). Routledge.

Archer, A. L., Gleason, M. M., & Vachon, V. L. (2003). Decoding and fluency: Foundational skills for struggling older readers. *Learning Disability Quarterly, 26*(2), 89–101. https://doi.org/10.2307/1593592

Ash, G. E., Kuhn, M. R., & Walpole, S. (2009). Analyzing "inconsistencies" in practice: teachers' continued use of round robin reading. *Reading & Writing Quarterly, 25*(1), 87–103.

Atkinson, J. W. (1957). Motivational determinants of risk-taking behavior. *Psychological Review, 64*(6), 359–372. 10.1037/h0043445.

Atkinson, R. K., Catrambone, R., & Merrill, M. M. (2003). Aiding transfer in statistics: Examining the use of conceptually oriented equations and elaborations during subgoal learning. *Journal of Educational Psychology, 95*, 762–773.

Ausubel, D. (1968). *Educational psychology: A cognitive view.* Holt, Rinehart & Winston.

Balthazar, C. H., & Scott, C. M. (2024). Sentences are key: Helping school-age children and adolescents build sentence skills needed for real language. *American Journal of Speech-Language Pathology, 33*(2), 564–579.

Bandura, A. (1977). Self-efficacy: Toward a unifying theory of behavioral change. *Psychological Review, 84*(2), 191.

Baneng, M. (2020). Cooperative learning approach applying Jigsaw strategy to enhance students' comprehension skill. *Journal of Physics, 1471*, 12027. https://doi.org/10.1088/1742-6596/1471/1/012027

Bardeen, M. G., & Lederman, L. M. (1998). Coherence in science education. *Science, 281*, 178–179.

Barth, A. E., & Elleman, A. (2017). Evaluating the impact of a multistrategy inference intervention for middle-grade struggling readers. *Language, Speech, and Hearing Services in Schools, 48*(1), 31–41.

Bassi, M., Steca, P., Fave, A. D., & Caprara, G. V. (2007). Academic self-efficacy beliefs and quality of experience in learning. *Journal of Youth & Adolescence, 36*(3), 301–312.

Baye, A., Inns, A., Lake, C., & Slavin, R. E. (2019). A synthesis of quantitative research on reading programs for secondary students. *Reading Research Quarterly, 54*(2), 133–166.

Beck, I., & McKeown, M. (1991). Conditions of vocabulary acquisition. In R. Barr, M. L. Kamil, P. B. Mosenthal, & P. D. Pearson (Eds.), *Handbook of reading research* (Vol. 2, pp. 789–814). Lawrence Erlbaum Associates.

Beck, I., McKeown, M., & Kucan, L. (2013). *Bringing words to life* (2nd ed.). Guilford.

Berry, A. (2022). *Reimagining student engagement: From disrupting to driving.* Corwin.

Bhattacharya, A. (2020). Syllabic versus morphemic analyses: Teaching multisyllabic word reading to older struggling readers. *Journal of Adolescent & Adult Literacy, 63*, 491–497.

Bowers, P. N., & Kirby, J. R. (2010). Effects of morphological instruction on vocabulary acquisition. *Reading & Writing, 23*(5), 515–537.

Brimo, D., Apel, K., & Fountain, T. (2017). Examining the contributions of syntactic awareness and syntactic knowledge to reading comprehension. *Journal of Research in Reading, 40*(1), 57–74. https://doi.org/10.1111/1467-9817.12050

Brod, G. (2021). Generative learning: Which strategies for what age? *Educational Psychology Review, 33*(4), 1295–1318. https://doi.org/10.1007/s10648-020-09571-9

Brody, S. (2001). *Teaching reading language, letters & thought* (2nd ed.). LARC.

Brown, J. I. (1947). Reading and vocabulary: 14 master words. In M. J. Herzberg (Ed.), *Word study* (pp. 1–4). G & C Merriam.

Burton, N. W., Welsh, C., Kostin, I., van Essen, T. (2009). *Toward a definition of verbal reasoning in higher education*. Educational Testing Service. https://files.eric.ed.gov/fulltext/ED507807.pdf

Cantor, P., Osher, D., Berg, J., Steyer, L., & Rose, T. (2019). Malleability, plasticity, and individuality: How children learn and develop in context. *Applied Developmental Science, 23*(4), 307–337. 10.1080/10888691.2017.1398649

Cantrell, S. C., Rintamaa, M., Anderman, E. M., & Anderman, L. H. (2018). Rural adolescents' reading motivation, achievement and behavior across transition to high school. *Journal of Educational Research, 111*(4), 417–428.

Chew, S. L., & Cerbin, W. J. (2021). The cognitive challenges of effective teaching. *The Journal of Economic Education, 52*(1), 17–40.

Clark, R. E., & Saxberg, B. (2018). Engineering motivation using the belief-control-expectancy framework. *Interdisciplinary Education and Psychology, 2*(1), 1–26.

Colón, J. (1961). *A Puerto Rican in New York and other sketches*. International Publishing.

Colquitt, J. A., LePine, J. A., & Noe, R. A. (2000). Toward an integrative theory of training motivation: A meta-analytic path analysis of 20 years of research. *Journal of Applied Psychology, 85*(5), 678–707.

Coxhead, A. (2000). A new academic word list. *TESOL Quarterly, 34*(2), 213–238.

Csikszentmihalyi, M. (1990). *Flow: The psychology of optimal experience*. Harper & Row.

Daniel, J., Capin, P., & Steinle, P. (2021). A synthesis of the sustainability of remedial reading intervention effects for struggling adolescent readers. *Journal of Learning Disabilities, 54*(3), 170–186.

Daniel, J., Vaughn, S., Roberts, G., & Grills, A. (2022). The importance of baseline word reading skills in examining student response to a multicomponent reading intervention. *Journal of Learning Disabilities, 55*(4), 259–271.

Dehaene, S. (2009). *Reading in the brain: The new science of how we learn to read*. Penguin.

Denton, C. A., Wexler, J., Vaughn, S., & Bryan, D. (2008). Intervention provided to linguistically diverse middle school students with severe reading difficulties. *Learning Disabilities Research & Practice, 23*(2), 79–89.

Diliberto, J. A., Beattie, J. R., Flowers, C. P., & Algozzine, R. F. (2009). Effects of teaching syllable skills instruction on reading achievement in struggling middle school readers. *Literacy Research & Instruction, 48*(1), 14–27.

Donegan, R. E., & Wanzek, J. (2021). Effects of reading interventions implemented for upper elementary struggling readers: A look at recent research. *Reading & Writing, 34*(8), 1943–1977.

Dweck, C. S. (2007). *Mindset: The new psychology of success*. Ballantine.

Ehri, L. C. (2014). Orthographic mapping in the acquisition of sight word reading, spelling memory, and vocabulary learning. *Scientific Studies of Reading, 18*(1), 5–21. https://doi.org/10.1080/10888438.2013.819356

Elbro, C., & Buch-Iversen, I. (2013). Activation of background knowledge for inference making: Effects on reading comprehension. *Scientific Studies of Reading, 17*(6), 435–452.

Elleman, A. M. (2017). Examining the impact of inference instruction on the literal and inferential comprehension of skilled and less skilled readers: A meta-analytic review. *Journal of Educational Psychology, 109*(6), 761–781.

Elleman, A. M., Lindo E. J., Murphy P., Compton D. L. (2009). The impact of vocabulary instruction on passage-level comprehension of school-age children: A meta-analysis. *Journal of Research on Educational Effectiveness, 2*, 1–44.

Elleman, A. M., Oslund, E. L., Griffin, N. M., & Myers, K. E. (2019). A review of middle school vocabulary interventions: Five research-based recommendations for practice. *Language, Speech & Hearing Services in Schools, 50*(4), 477–492.

Fang, Z. (2006). The language demands of science reading in middle school. *International Journal of Science Education, 28*(5), 491–520. https://doi.org/10.1080/09500690500339092

Fearn, L., & Farnan, N. (2001). *Interactions: Teaching writing and the language arts*. Allyn & Bacon.

Fernandes, M. A., Wammes, J. D., & Meade, M. E. (2018). The surprisingly powerful influence of drawing on memory. *Current Directions in Psychological Science, 27*(5), 302–308. https://doi.org/10.1177/0963721418755385

Ferrer-Caja, E., & Weiss, M. R. (2002). Cross-validation of a model of intrinsic motivation with students enrolled in high school elective courses. *Journal of Experimental Education, 71*(1), 41–65.

Filderman, M. J., Austin, C. R., Boucher, A. N., O'Donnell, K., & Swanson, E. A. (2022). A meta-analysis of the effects of reading comprehension interventions on the reading comprehension outcomes of struggling readers in third through 12th grades. *Exceptional Children, 88*(2), 163–184.

Fillmore, L. W., & Fillmore, C. J. (n.d.). What does text complexity mean for English learners and language minority students? *Understanding Language Project.* Stanford University. https://ul.stanford.edu/sites/default/files/resource/2021-12/06-LWF%20CJF%20Text%20Complexity%20FINAL_0.pdf

Fiorella, L. (2023). Making sense of generative learning. *Educational Psychology Review, 35*(50), 1–42. https://doi.org/10.1007/s10648-023-09769-7

Fiorella, L., & Mayer, R. E. (2015). Learning as a generative activity: Eight learning strategies that promote understanding. *Cambridge University Press.* https://doi.org/10.1017/CBO9781107707085

Fish, S. (2012). *How to write a sentence and how to read one.* Harper.

Fisher, D., & Frey, N. (2007). *Scaffolded writing instruction: Teaching with a gradual-release framework.* Scholastic.

Fisher, D., & Frey, N. (2010). *Guided instruction: How to develop confident and successful learners.* ASCD.

Fisher, D., & Frey, N. (2014). Close reading as an intervention for struggling middle school readers. *Journal of Adolescent & Adult Literacy, 57*(5), 367–376.

Fisher, D., & Frey, N. (2015). Teacher modeling using complex informational texts. *Reading Teacher, 69*(1), 63–69.

Fisher, D., & Frey, N. (2019). Teacher credibility in literacy learning. *Journal of Adolescent and Adult Literacy, 63*(3), 356–359.

Fisher, D., & Frey, N. (2023). *The vocabulary playbook: Learning words that matter, K–12.* Corwin.

Fisher, D., Frey, N., Almarode, J., Barbee, K., Amador, O., & Assof, J. (2024). *Teacher clarity playbook* (2nd ed.). Corwin.

Fisher, D., Frey, N., & Lapp, D. (2010). Responding when students don't get it. *Journal of Adolescent & Adult Literacy, 54,* 56–60.

Fisher, D., Frey, N., & Lapp, D. (2023). *Teaching reading: A playbook for developing skilled readers through word recognition and language comprehension.* Corwin.

Flavell, J. H. (1979). Metacognition and cognitive monitoring. A new area of cognitive-development inquiry. *American Psychologist, 34*(10), 906–911.

Fong, C. J., Gonzales, C., Hill-Troglin Cox, C., & Shinn, H. B. (2023). Academic help-seeking and achievement of postsecondary students: A meta-analytic investigation. *Journal of Educational Psychology, 115*(1), 1–21.

Frayer, D. A., Frederick, W. C., & Klausmeier, H. J. (1969). *A schema for testing the level of concept mastery* (Working paper no. 16). Madison: University of Wisconsin.

Frey, N., & Fisher, D. (2013). *Rigorous reading: 5 access points for comprehending complex texts.* Corwin.

Frey, N., Fisher, D., & Almarode, J. (2023). *How scaffolding works: A playbook for supporting and releasing responsibility to students.* Corwin.

Frishkoff, G. A., Perfetti, C. A., & Collins-Thompson, K. (2011). Predicting robust vocabulary growth from measures of incremental learning. *Scientific Studies of Reading, 15*(1), 71–91.

Goldman, S. R., Britt, M. A., Brown, W., Cribb, G., George, M., Greenleaf, C., Lee, C. D., Shanahan, C., & Project READI. (2016). Disciplinary literacies and learning to read for understanding: A conceptual framework for disciplinary literacy. *Educational Psychologist, 51*(2), 219–246.

Graham, S., Kim, Y.-S., Cao, Y., Lee, J. won, Tate, T., Collins, P., Cho, M., Moon, Y., Chung, H. Q., & Olson, C. B. (2023). A meta-analysis of writing treatments for students in grades 6–12. *Journal of Educational Psychology, 115*(7), 1004–1027.

Haitian Revolution. (2024, May 3). In *Wikipedia.* https://en.wikipedia.org/wiki/Haitian_Revolution

Hall, C., Roberts, G., Cho, E., Mcculley, L., Carroll, M., & Vaughn, S. (2017). Reading instruction for English learners in the middle grades: A meta-analysis. *Educational Psychology Review, 29*(4), 763–794.

Hattan, C., & Alexander, P. A. (2021). The effects of knowledge activation training on rural middle-school students' expository text comprehension: A mixed-methods study. *Journal of Educational Psychology, 113*(5), 879–897.

Hattie, J. (2023). *Visible learning: The sequel. A synthesis of over 2100 meta-analyses relating to achievement.* Routledge.

Hattie, J., & Yates, G. C. R. (2014). *Visible learning and the science of how we learn.* Routledge.

He, J., Liu, Y., Ran, T., & Zhang, D. (2023). How students' perception of feedback influences self-regulated learning: The mediating role of self-efficacy and goal orientation. *European Journal of Psychology of Education, 38*(4), 1551–1569.

Henry, M. (2017). Morphemes matter: A framework for instruction. *Perspectives on Language and Literacy, 43*(7), 23–26.

Hidayati, F., & Rohayati, D. (2017). The effectiveness of jigsaw on reading comprehension of analytical exposition text. *Journal of Applied Linguistics and*

Literacy, 1(2), 1–9. https://doi.org/10.25157/jall
.v1i2.1732

Hill, K. (2020). "Did my heart love till now?": Transforming *Romeo and Juliet* and readers through choral reading. *English Journal, 109*(4), 31–37.

Hinton, S. E. (1967). *The outsiders*. Viking.

Hole, J. L., & Crozier, W. R. (2007). Dispositional and situational learning goals and children's self-regulation. *British Journal of Educational Psychology, 77*(4), 773–786.

Hudson, R. (2016). Grammar instruction. In C. A. MacArthur, S. Graham, & J. Fitzgerald (Eds.), *Handbook of writing research* (2nd ed., pp. 288–299). Guilford.

Jang, B. G., & Ryoo, J. H. (2019). Multiple dimensions of adolescents' reading attitudes and their relationship with reading comprehension. *Reading & Writing, 32*(7), 1769–1793.

Jeno, L. M., Nylehn, J., Hole, T. N., Raaheim, A., Velle, G., & Vandvik, V. (2023). Motivational determinants of students' academic functioning: The role of autonomy-support, autonomous motivation, and perceived competence. *Scandinavian Journal of Educational Research, 67*(2), 194–211.

Kerns, D. (2020). Does English have useful syllable division patterns? *Reading Research Quarterly, 55*(S1), S145–S160. 10.1002/rrq.342

Kidron, Y., & Lindsay, J. (2014). *The effects of increased learning time on student academic and nonacademic outcomes: Findings from a meta-analytic review* (REL 2014-015). Washington, DC: Regional Educational Laboratory Appalachia, National Center for Education Evaluation and Regional Assistance, Institute of Education Sciences, U.S. Department of Education.

Kilpatrick, D. A. (2015). *Essentials of assessing, preventing, and overcoming reading difficulties*. John Wiley and Sons.

Kilpatrick, D. A. (2016). *Equipped for reading success: A comprehensive, step-by-step program for developing phonemic awareness and fluency word recognition*. Casey & Kirsch Publishers.

Kintsch, W. (1998). *Comprehension: A paradigm for cognition*. Cambridge.

Kirschner, P. A., & Hendrick, C. (2020). *How learning works: Seminal works in educational psychology and what they mean in practice*. Routledge.

Klauer, K. J., & Phye, G. D. (2008). Inductive reasoning: A training approach. *Review of Educational Research, 78*(1), 85–123. https://doi.org/
10.3102/0034654307313402

Krepel, A., de Bree, E. H., & de Jong, P. F. (2021). Does the availability of orthography support L2 word learning? *Reading & Writing, 34*(2), 467–496.

Kuhn, M. R., & Schwanenflugel, P. J. (2019). Prosody, pacing, and situational fluency (or why fluency matters for older readers). *Journal of Adolescent & Adult Literacy, 62*(4), 363– 368. https://doi.org/
10.1002/jaal.867

LaBerge, D., & Samuels, S. J. (1974). Toward a theory of automatic information processing in reading. *Cognitive Psychology, 6*, 293–323.

Landreth, S. J., & Young, C. (2021). Developing fluency and comprehension with the secondary fluency routine. *Journal of Educational Research, 114*(3), 252–262.

Lee, J., & Yoon, S. Y. (2017). The effects of repeated reading on reading fluency for students with reading disabilities: A meta-analysis. *Journal of Learning Disabilities, 50*(2), 213–224.

Lesaux, N. K., Kieffer, M. J., Faller, S. E., & Kelley, J. G. (2010). The effectiveness and ease of implementation of an academic vocabulary intervention for linguistically diverse students in urban middle schools. *Reading Research Quarterly, 45*(2), 196–228.

Livingston, D. (May 25, 2016). *Lift off*. Harvard Graduate School of Education. https://www.gse.harvard.edu/
ideas/news/16/05/lift

Lovett, M. W., Frijters, J. C., Steinbach, K. A., De Palma, M., Lacerenza, L., Wolf, M., Sevcik, R. A., & Morris, R. D. (2022). Interpreting comprehension outcomes after multiple-component reading intervention for children and adolescents with reading disabilities. *Learning & Individual Differences, 100*. https://doi.org/10.1016/j
.lindif.2022.102224

Lovett, M. W., Frijters, J. C., Steinbach, K. A., Sevcik, R. A., & Morris, R. D. (2021). Effective intervention for adolescents with reading disabilities: Combining reading and motivational remediation to improve outcomes. *Journal of Educational Psychology, 113*(4), 656–689.

Lupo, S. M., Berry, A., Thacker, E., Sawyer, A., & Merritt, J. (2020). Rethinking text sets to support knowledge building and interdisciplinary learning. *The Reading Teacher, 73*(4), 513–524.

Lupo, S. M., Tortorelli, L., Invernizzi, M., Ryoo, J. H., & Strong, J. Z. (2019). An exploration of text difficulty and knowledge support on adolescents' comprehension. *Reading Research Quarterly, 54*(4), 457–479.

Lupo, S. M., & Tortorelli, L. (2017, December). *What the doctor orders: What texts are we prescribing to our struggling readers?* Paper presented at the annual meeting of the Literacy Research Association, Tampa, FL.

Magliano, J. P., Talwar, A., Feller, D. P., Wang, Z., O'Reilly, T., & Sabatini, J. (2023). Exploring thresholds in the foundational skills for reading and comprehension outcomes in the context of postsecondary readers. *Journal of Learning Disabilities, 56*(1), 43–57.

Maier, S. F., & Seligman, M. E. P. (1976). Learned helplessness: Theory and evidence. *Journal of Experimental Psychology: General, 105*(1), 3–46. https://doi.org/10.1037/0096-3445.105.1.3

Malik, S. A. (2017). Revisiting and re-representing scaffolding: The two-gradient model. *Cogent Education, 4*(1), 1–13.

Malkus, N. (2024). *Long COVID for public schools: Chronic absenteeism before and after the pandemic.* American Enterprise Institute. https://www.aei.org/wp-content/uploads/2024/01/Long-COVID-for-Public-Schools.pdf?x85095

Margulieux, L. E., & Catrambone, R. (2021). Scaffolding problem solving with learners' own self explanations of subgoals. *Journal of Computing in Higher Education, 33*(2), 499–523.

Marzano, R. J., & Pickering, D. J. (2005). *Building academic vocabulary: Teacher's manual.* ASCD.

McCarthy, K. S., Guerrero, T. A., Kent, K. M., Allen, L. K., McNamara, D. S., Chao, S.-F., Steinberg, J., O'Reilly, T., & Sabatini, J. (2018). Comprehension in a scenario-based assessment: Domain and topic-specific background knowledge. *Discourse Processes, 55*(5/6), 510–524.

McEwan, E. K. (2007). *40 ways to support struggling readers in content classrooms: Grades 6–12.* Corwin.

McVee, M. B., Dunsmore, K., & Gavelek, J. R. (2005). Schema theory revisited. *Review of Educational Research, 75*, 531–566.

Methe, S. A., & Hintze, J. M. (2003). Evaluating teacher modeling as a strategy to increase student reading behavior. *School Psychology Review, 32*(4), 617–623.

Moore, D. W., Alvermann, D. E., & Hinchman, K. A. (2000). *Struggling adolescent readers: A collection of teaching strategies.* International Reading Association.

Nagy, W. E., & Anderson, R. C. (1984). How many words are there in printed school English? *Reading Research Quarterly, 19*, 303–330.

Nagy, W. E., Anderson, R. C., & Herman, P. A. (1987). Learning word meanings from context during normal reading. *American Educational Research Journal, 24*, 237–270.

Nagy, W. E., & Scott, J. A. (2000). Vocabulary processes. In M. Kamil, P. Mosenthal, P. D. Pearson, & R. Barr (Eds.), *Handbook of reading research* (Vol. 3, pp. 269–284). Lawrence Erlbaum.

Namaziandost, E., Gilakjani, A. P., & Hidayatullah. (2020). Enhancing pre-intermediate EFL learners' reading comprehension through the use of Jigsaw technique. *Cogent Arts & Humanities, 7*(1). https://doi.org/10.1080/23311983.2020.1738833

Nanda, A. O., Greenberg, D., & Morris, R. (2010). Modeling child-based theoretical reading constructs with struggling adult readers. *Journal of Learning Disabilities, 43*, 139–153.

National Academies of Sciences, Engineering, and Medicine. (2012). *A framework for K–12 science education: Practices, crosscutting concepts, and core ideas.* Washington, DC: The National Academies Press. https://doi.org/10.17226/13165

National Behaviour Support Service. (n.d.). KWL charts: Reading and learning strategy.

National Center for Educational Progress. (March 2024). *Reading assessment 2022.* https://nces.ed.gov/nationsreportcard/reading/

National Institute of Child Health and Human Development, NIH, DHHS. (2000). *Report of the National Reading Panel: Teaching children to read: Reports of the subgroups* (00-4754). Washington, DC: U.S. Government Printing Office.

National Research Council. (2000). *How people learn: Brain, mind, experience, and school.* In J. D. Bransford, A. L. Brown, & R. Cocking (Eds.), *Commission on behavioral and social sciences and education.* National Academy Press.

Nomi, T. (2015). "Double-dose" English as a strategy for improving adolescent literacy: Total effect and mediated effect through classroom peer ability change. *Social Science Research, 52*, 716–739.

Ogle, D. M. (1986). K-W-L: A teaching model that develops active reading of expository text. *Reading Teacher, 39*(6), 564–570. https://doi.org/10.1598/RT.39.6.11

Ogle, D. M., Blachowicz, C., Fisher, P., & Lang, L. (2015). *Academic vocabulary in middle and high school: Effective practices across disciplines.* Guilford.

Opatz, M. O., & Kocherhans, S. (2024). Using a supplemental, multicomponent reading intervention to increase adolescent readers' achievement. *Journal of Adolescent & Adult Literacy, 67,* 294–302.

OpenAI. (2023). *ChatGPT* (Mar 14 version) [Large language model]. https://chat.openai.com/chat

Oslund, E. L., Clemens, N. H., Simmons, D. C. (2018). The direct and indirect effects of word reading comprehension: Comparing struggling and adequate comprehenders. *Reading & Writing, 31*(2), 355–379.

Ozuru, Y., Dempsey, K., & McNamara, D. S. (2009). Prior knowledge, reading skill, and text cohesion in the comprehension of science texts. *Learning and Instruction, 19*(3), 228–242. https://doi.org/10.1016/j.learninstruc.2008.04.003

Paige, D. D., Rasinski, T., Magpuri-Lavell, T., & Smith, G. S. (2014). Interpreting the relationships among prosody, automaticity, accuracy, and silent reading comprehension in secondary students. *Journal of Literacy Research, 46*(2), 123–156. https://doi.org/10.1177/1086296X14535170

Paris, S. G. (2005). Reinterpreting the development of reading skills. *Reading Research Quarterly, 40*(2), 184–202.

Peng, P., Wang, W., Filderman, M. J., Zhang, W., & Lin, L. (2024). The active ingredient in reading comprehension strategy intervention for struggling readers: A Bayesian network meta-analysis. *Review of Educational Research, 94*(2), 228–267. https://doi.org/10.3102/00346543231171345

Perfetti, C. A., & Stafura, J. (2014). Word knowledge in a theory of reading comprehension. *Scientific Studies of Reading, 18*(1), 22–37. https://doi.org/10.1080/10888438.2013.827687

Petscher, Y., Cabell, S. Q., Catts, H. W., Compton, D. L., Foorman, B. R., Hart, S. A., Lonigan, C. J., Phillips, B. M., Schatschneider, C., Steacy, L. M., Terry, N. P., & Wagner, R. K. (2020). How the science of reading informs 21st-century education. *Reading Research Quarterly, 55*(S1), S267–S282. https://doi.org/10.1002/rrq.352

Pikulski, J. J., & Chard, D. J. (2005). Fluency: Bridge between decoding and reading comprehension. *Reading Teacher, 58*(6), 510–519.

Pintrich, P. R. (2003). A motivational science perspective on the role of student motivation in learning and teaching contexts. *Journal of Educational Psychology, 95,* 667–686.

Purcell-Gates, V., Duke, N., & Stouffer, J. (2016). Teaching literacy: Reading. In D. H. Gitomer & C. A. Bell (Eds.), *Handbook of research on teaching* (5th ed., pp. 1217–1268). American Educational

Research Association. http://www.jstor.org/stable/j.ctt1s474hg.25

Rasinski, T. V., Chang, S.-C., Edmondson, E., Nageldinger, J., Nigh, J., Remark, L., Kenney, K. S., Walsh-Moorman, E., Yildirim, K., Nichols, W. D., Paige, D. D., & Rupley, W. H. (2017). Reading fluency and college readiness. *Journal of Adolescent & Adult Literacy, 60*(4), 453–460.

Reardon, S. F., Valentino, R. A., Shores, K. A. (2012). Patterns of literacy among U.S. students. *The Future of Children, 22*(2), 17–38.

Recht, D. R., & Leslie, L. (1988). Effect of prior knowledge on good and poor readers' memory of text. *Journal of Educational Psychology, 80*(1), 16–20. https://doi.org/10.1037/0022-0663.80.1.16

Rege, M., Hanselman, P., Solli, I. F., Dweck, C. S., Ludvigsen, S., Bettinger, E., Crosnoe, R., Muller, C., Walton, G., Duckworth, A., & Yeager, D. S. (2021). How can we inspire nations of learners? An investigation of growth mindset and challenge-seeking in two countries. *American Psychologist, 76*(5), 755–767.

Reynolds, D., & Goodwin, A. (2016). Supporting students reading complex texts: Evidence for motivational scaffolding. *AERA Open, 2*(4). https://doi.org/10.1177/2332858416680353

Richards-Tutor, C., Baker, D. L., Gersten, R., Baker, S. K., & Smith, J. M. (2016). The effectiveness of reading interventions for English learners. *Exceptional Children, 82*(2), 144–169.

Ritchhart, R., & Church, M. (2020). *The power of making thinking visible: Practices to engage and empower all learners.* Jossey-Bass.

Rodriguez, L. (2005). *Always running: Me vida loca: Gang days in L.A.* Atria.

Rosenshine, B. (2012) Principles of instruction: Research-based strategies that all teachers should know. *American Educator, 36*(1), 12–39.

Rothkopf, E. Z. (2008). Reflections on the field: Aspirations of learning science and the practical logic of instructional enterprises. *Educational Psychology Review, 20*(3), 351–368.

Rumelhart, D. E. (1984). Schemata and the cognitive system. In R. S. Wyer & T. K. Srull, *Handbook of social cognition* (pp. 161–188). Lawrence Erlbaum.

Saddler, B., Ellis-Robinson, T., & Asaro-Saddler, K. (2018). Using sentence combining instruction to enhance the writing skills of children with learning disabilities. *Learning Disabilities: A Contemporary Journal, 16*(2), 191–202.

Sadler, P. M., & Tai, R. H. (2007). The two high school pillars supporting college science. *Science, 317,* 457–458.

Samuels, J., & Decker, S. L. (2023). Neurocognitive constructs as longitudinal predictors of reading fluency. *Psychology in the Schools, 60*(10), 3920–3946.

Sandilos, L. E., Rimm, K. S. E., & Cohen, J. J. (2017). Warmth and demand: The relation between students' perceptions of the classroom environment and achievement growth. *Child Development, 88*(4), 1321–1337.

Sawchuck, S. (2024, January 15). *Reading comprehension challenges and opportunities, in charts.* EdWeek Research Center. https://www.edweek.org/teaching-learning/reading-comprehension-challenges-and-opportunities-in-charts/2024/01

Scammacca, N., Robers, G., Vaughn, S., Edmonds, M., Wexler, J., Reutebuch, C. K., Klein, C., & Torgesen, J. K. (2007). *Intervention for adolescent struggling readers: A meta- analysis with implication for practice.* RMC Research Corporation, Center on Instruction.

Schleppegrell, M. J. (2001). Linguistic features of the language of schooling. *Linguistics and Education, 12*(4), 431–459. https://doi.org/10.1016/S0898-5898(01)00073-0

Sedita, J. (2009). *The key vocabulary routine.* Keys to Literacy.

Shanahan, T. (2019, September 28). *Five things every teacher should know about vocabulary instruction.* Literacy Blog. https://www.shanahanonliteracy.com

Shanahan, T. (2022, August 13). *Trying again: What teachers need to know about sentence comprehension.* Literacy Blog. https://www.shanahanonliteracy.com

Shernoff, D. J., Csikszentmihalyi, M. Schneider, B., & Shernoff, E. S. (2003). Student engagement in high school classrooms from the perspective of flow theory. *School Psychology Quarterly, 18*(2), 158–176.

Silver, H. F., Abla, C., & Boutz, A. L. (2018). *Tools for classroom instruction that works.* Thoughtful Education Press.

Simonsmeier, B. A., Flaig, M., Deiglmayr, A., Schalk, L., & Schneider, M. (2022). Domain-specific prior knowledge and learning: A meta-analysis. *Educational Psychologist, 57*(1), 31–54.

Stanovich, K. E. (1986). The Matthew effects in reading: Some consequences of individual differences in the acquisition of literacy. *Reading Research Quarterly, 21*(4), 360–407.

Student Achievement Partners. (n.d.). *Juicy sentence guidance.* https://achievethecore.org/content/upload/Juicy%20Sentence%20Guidance.pdf

Taba, H. (1967). *Teacher's handbook for elementary social studies.* Addison-Wesley.

Taft, M., & Krebs-Lazendic, L. (2013). The role of orthographic syllable structure in assigning letters to their position in visual word recognition. *Journal of Memory & Language, 68*(2), 85–97.

Tarchi, C. (2010). Reading comprehension of informative texts in secondary school: A focus on direct and indirect effects of reader's prior knowledge. *Learning & Individual Differences, 20*(5), 415–420.

Templeton, S. (1983). Using the spelling/meaning connection to develop word knowledge in older students. *Journal of Reading, 27*(1), 8–14.

Tighe, E., & Schatschneider, C. (2014a). Examining the relationships of component reading skills to reading comprehension in struggling adult readers: A meta-analysis. *Journal of Learning Disabilities, 49*(4), 395–409.

Tighe, E., & Schatschneider, C. (2014b). A dominance analysis approach to determining predictor importance in third, seventh, and tenth grade reading comprehension skills. *Reading & Writing, 27*(1), 101–127.

TNTP. (2018). *The opportunity myth: What students can show us about how school is letting them down—and how to fix it.* https://tntp.org/publication/the-opportunity-myth/

Tracy, B. (1996). *Accelerated learning techniques.* Nightingale-Conant.

Uchihara, T., Webb, S., & Yanagisawa, A. (2019). The effects of repetition on incidental vocabulary learning: A meta-analysis of correlational studies. *Language Learning, 69*(3), 559–599.

Van Gog, T, Kirschner, F., Kester, L., & Paas, F. (2012). Timing and frequency of mental effort measurement: Evidence in favour of repeated measures. *Applied Cognitive Psychology, 26*(6), 833–839.

Vaughn, S., Gersten, R., & Chard, D. J. (2000). The underlying message in LD intervention research: Findings from research syntheses. *Exceptional Children, 67*(1), 99–114.

Vaughn, S., Gersten, R., Dimino, J., Taylor, M. J., Newman-Gonchar, R., Krowka, S., Kieffer, M. J., McKeown, M., Reed, D., Sanchez, M., St. Martin, K., Wexler, J., Morgan, S., Yañez, A., & Jayanthi, M. (2022). *Providing reading interventions for students in grades 4–9. Educator's practice guide.* WWC 2022007. What Works Clearinghouse. https://files.eric.ed.gov/fulltext/ED617876.pdf

Vorstius, C., Radach, R., Mayer, M. B., & Lonigan, C. J. (2013). Monitoring local comprehension monitoring in sentence reading. *School Psychology Review, 42*(2), 191–206. https://doi.org/10.1080/02796015.2013.12087484

Walston, J., Rathbun, A. H., & Germino-Hausken, E. (2008). *Eighth grade: First findings from the final round of the early childhood longitudinal study, kindergarten class of 1998–99 (ECLS-K).* National Center for Education Statistics, U.S. Department of Education. https://nces.ed.gov/pubs2008/2008088.pdf

Wang, Z., Sabatini, J., O'Reilly, T., & Weeks, J. (2019). Decoding and reading comprehension: A test of the decoding threshold hypothesis. *Journal of Educational Psychology, 111*(3), 387–401. https://doi.org/10.1037/edu0000302

Washburn, J. (2023). Monitoring reading component skills during a word-level intervention for adolescents with limited reading proficiency. *Learning Disabilities Research & Practice, 38*(2), 155–172.

Weiner, B. (1985). An attributional theory of achievement, motivation, and emotion. *Psychological Review, 92*(4), 548–573.

Wexler, J., Vaughn, S., Edmonds, M., & Reutebuch, C. K. (2008). A synthesis of fluency interventions for secondary struggling readers. *Reading & Writing, 21*(4), 317–347.

White, T. G., Sowell, J., & Yanagihara, A. (1989). Teaching elementary students to use word-part clues. *The Reading Teacher, 42,* 302–308.

Williams, R. L., & Eggert, A. C. (2002). Notetaking predictors of test performance. *Teaching of Psychology, 29,* 234–237.

Willingham, D. T. (2021). *Why don't students like school? A cognitive scientist answers questions about how the mind works and what it means for your classroom* (2nd ed). Jossey-Bass.

Wolters, C., Denton, C., York, M., & Francis, D. (2014). Adolescents' motivation for reading: Group differences and relation to standardized achievement. *Reading & Writing, 27*(3), 503–533.

Worthy, J., & Broaddus K. (2001/2002). Fluency beyond the primary grades: From group performance to silent, independent reading. *The Reading Teacher, 55,* 334–343.

Wright, T. S., & Cervetti, G. N. (2017). A systematic review of the research on vocabulary instruction that impacts text comprehension. *Reading Research Quarterly, 52*(2), 203–226.

Zinn, H. (2023). *A young people's history of the United States* (revised and updated). Triangle Square.

Zwiers, J., & Crawford, M. (2011). *Academic conversations: Classroom talk that fosters critical thinking and content understandings.* Stenhouse.

Index

Academic
  failure, 14
  success, 14–15, 61
  vocabulary, 83, 125, 126
Academic language building
  affinity mapping, 94–95
  hexagonal thinking, 93–94
  routines, 92–93
  word wall, 95–96
Accessible informational texts, 50, 51
Activated background knowledge
  mark my confusion, 54
  self-questioning, 53–54
Activate dialogue, 132–134
Activating prior knowledge
  anticipation guides, 48–49
  initial assessments, 45–46
  language charts, 46–48
Adolescent literacy, 7, 13. *See also* Self-efficacy
Adolescent readers, 7
  background knowledge on, 33–58
  educators of, 2
  foundational skills, 5, 167–168
  MCRI programs, 9, 144, 149, 150, 158, 161, 164
  morphological awareness, 99
Adolescent reading components, 143
  background knowledge, 33–58
  self-efficacy, 11–32
  sentence analysis, 101–117
  verbal reasoning, 119–140
  word recognition, 59–78
Advance organizers, 52
Affinity mapping, 94–95
Always Running: Mi Vida Loca (Rodriguez), 115
Anderson, R. C., 81, 83
Anticipation guides, 48–49
Armed Services Vocational Aptitude Battery
  (ASVAB), 121
Arm-tapping strategy, 69–71, 77
Ash, G. E., 60
Aspiring readers, 142, 143, 146, 152, 163, 164

Automaticity, 64, 140
  sight-word, 78
  in word recognition, 141–165
Avoiding learning, 17, 19

Background knowledge, 58, 120
  activating prior knowledge, 45–49
  adolescent readers, 35
  the baseball study, 35
  building, 50–53
  conditionalized, 40–42
  instruction, 122–123
  KIP, 34
  K-W-L, 54, 56–57
  new learning, 37
  organized, 38–40
  students to activate, 53–54
  transferable, 42–44
  useable, 36–44
Balthazar, C. H., 102
Beck, I., 81, 90
Brokaw, E., 54
Brown, J. I., 85
Bruner, 121
Building background knowledge
  advance organizer, 52
  quad text sets, 50–51
  short recaps, 53
  targeted search term, 51

Cerbin, W. J., 23, 26
Challenge texts, 51, 55
Chew, S. L., 23, 26
Choral reading
  public performance element, 66
  science teachers, 67
  whole class, 74–77
Close reading
  annotation schemes, 113
  description, 111
  qualitative factors, text complexity, 112

179

questions, 113–117
text selection, 112
Cognates, 85
Cognitive barriers
description, 23
identification, student interview, 25
learning, 24
survey questions, 26
Cognitive load, 123
Cognitive psychology, 142
Colón, J., 40
Comprehension, 35–36. *See also* Reading
comprehension
Concept maps, 52, 90, 131
Conditionalized learning, 40–42
Connect-extend-challenge, 134
Crawford, M., 133
Critical thinking, 125
Cues, 137, 157

Daniel, J., 144
Direct instruction, 69, 70, 91, 145, 151, 152
Direct word learning, 82
Discussion roundtable, 134
Disruptions, 19
Driving, 21

Education Testing Service (ETS), 123, 124
EdWeek Research Center, 122
Elleman, A. M., 82

Fang, Z., 104
Fillmore, C. J., 106
Fillmore, L. W., 106
Fiorella, L., 131
Fish, S., 102
Fisher, D., 96
Five-day fluency routine, 72–73
Five-word summary, 133
Flexible word chunking, 77
adjust vowel sounds, 72
segment word parts, 71–72
Florida Center for Reading Research, 159
Fluency, reading
automaticity, 64
building, 72–73
choral reading, 66–67
oral reading assessments, 158
phrase progressions, 159–160
prosody, 65–66, 158
Read This to Me strategy, 73–74

repeated readings, 66–67, 158–159
roll the inference, 160–161
situational, 65
teacher modeling, 67
ten-minute daily fluency routine, 76
word recognition, 64–67
Foundational Reading Skills Assessment, 147, 149
Frey, N., 96

Generative-learning activities (GLA)
enacting, 132
explaining, 132
types of, 131
visualizing, 131–132
Generative sentences
benefits, 110
prompts and examples, 111
GLA. *See* Generative-learning activities (GLA)
Grammar, 66, 103, 105, 106, 117, 168
Graphemes, 151, 152
Graphic organizers, 18, 22, 39, 52, 97–99

Hattie, J., 132
Hexagonal thinking, 93–94
Hinton, S. E., 161
Hooks and Bridges technique, 48
How People Learn: Brain, Mind, Experience, and School
(National Research Council's report), 37

"I can" statements, 138
Indirect word learning, 82
Informational texts, 50, 51
Initial assessments, 45–46
International Phonetic Alphabet, 80
Intervention, 169
adolescent reading, 143–144
aspiring readers, 142, 143, 146, 152, 163, 164
characteristics, reading, 144–145
content and instruction, tutoring, 150–151
effective tutoring sessions, 145
explicit instruction, 152–157
fluency, 158–161
frequency and duration, tutoring, 149–150
identification of students, tutoring, 146–148
MCRI programs, 144, 164
morphology and word study, 161–163
passage reading of complex texts, 164
RISE assessment, 143
systematic instruction, 151–152
teacher credibility, 142
word recognition, 151–157

Investing, 21
"I" statements, 129

Jang, B. G., 142
Jigsaw protocol, 16–22
    avoiding learning, 19
    continuum of engagement, 16, 17
    disruptions, 19
    driving, 21
    expert group graphic organizer, 22
    instructions, teachers, 17–18
    investing, 21
    participation, 20
    withdrawing, 20
Juicy sentences
    routine, 106–108
    selection criteria, 108

Knowledge-building, 123–125, 161, 168
Knowledge is power (KIP), 34, 35
Know-want-learn (K-W-L) chart, 46–48, 54,
    56, 127
Kuhn, M. R., 65
K-W-L. *See* Know-want-learn (K-W-L) chart

Landreth, S. J., 72
Language
    building routines, 92–93
    charts, 46–48
    figurative, 21
    spoken interactions and school texts, 104
Learned helplessness, 12
Leslie, L., 35
Literacy research, 3–4, 9
Lupo, S. M., 125

MagicSchool.ai, 114
Master words, 85
Matthew effect, 14
McKeown, M., 90
MCRI programs. *See* Multicomponent reading
    invention (MCRI) programs
Measures of Academic Progress (MAP), 146
Metacognition, 54
    awareness, 65, 130, 137
    as cognitive barrier, 24, 26
    modeling, 128
    prompts, 139, 157
    reflective questioning, 128
    self-assessment, 137
    verbal reasoning, 129–131, 139

Miscues, 157
Morphemes, 82, 83, 85
Morphological awareness, word knowledge, 99
    cognates, 85
    high-utility prefixes, 84
    master words, Brown, 85
    morphemes, 83, 85
    terms, 86
Motivational texts, 50, 51
Multicomponent reading invention (MCRI) programs,
    9, 149, 161
    complex text passages, 164
    fluency-building, 158
    purpose, 144
    repeated readings, 158
    time distribution, 150
Multimodal texts, 50, 51
Multisyllabic words, 63–64, 68, 71, 72, 77, 80, 82, 83, 99,
    150, 152, 160, 163–165

Nagy, W. E., 81, 83
National Assessment of Educational Progress
    (NAEP), 2
National Endowment for the Arts, 169
National Research Council, 37, 39, 42
Negative emotions, 14
Neurotransmission, 33

Ogle, D. M., 82
Opatz, M. O, 164
Organized background knowledge, 38–40
Orthographic mapping, 62–64
The Outsiders (Hinton), 161

Participation level of engagement, 20
Passage reading of complex texts, 164
Phoneme, 151–152
Phoneme-grapheme correspondences, 151, 160
Phonics, 5, 62, 152–154, 156, 165
Phrase progressions, 159–160
Popcorn reading, 60
Prompts, 111, 134–137, 139, 157
Prosody, 65–66, 158–160
Purcell-Gates, V., 129

Quad text sets, 50–51

Reading comprehension
    challenges, 103–104
    easier-to-read texts, 125
    fluency, 64–66

grade-level ideas, 125–127
older readers, strategies for, 130
orthographic mapping, 62–64
sight words, 62
strategies, 122, 130
verbal reasoning, 119–139
word recognition, 62–64
Reading Inventory and Scholastic Evaluation (RISE)
assessment, 143
Read This to Me strategy, 73–74
Recht, D. R., 35
Repeated reading, 66–67, 158–159
Review in learning, 53
"Right church, wrong pew" phenomenon, 41
RISE assessment. *See* Reading Inventory and Scholastic
Evaluation (RISE) assessment
Rodriguez, L., 115
Romeo and Juliet (Shakespeare), 67
Rosenshine, B., 53
Round-robin reading, 60, 66
Rumelhart, D. E., 38, 40
Ryoo, J. H., 142

Sadler, P. M., 41
Scaffolds
asking robust questions, 135–136
cues, 137, 139
definition, 135
distributed, 135, 137
front-end, 137
learning station, 138
prompts, 136
regenerated texts, 135
Schema theory, 38
Schwanenflugel, P. J., 65
Scott, C. M., 102
Scott, J. A., 81
Self-assessment, 90
Self-efficacy, 167, 168
cognitive barriers, 23–26
continuum of engagement, 17
definition, 12
elephant training, traditional way of, 11–12
goal-setting, 13
levels of engagement, jigsaw protocol, 16–22
Matthew effect, 14
mental effort check-in, 28–29
motivation and success, 13–15
student responses, 29–30
student's values, 27–28
Self-questioning, 53–54

Self-regulation, 12, 16, 28, 78
Sentence analysis, 169
close reading, 111–117
cohesion, 102
generative sentences, 110–111
grammar, 103, 105
juicy sentences, 106–108
phrases and clauses, 103
science sentences, 104
sentence combining, 108–109, 117
sentence-level instruction, 102
spoken interactions and school texts, language
used, 104
syntax, 103
Sentence combining, 108–109, 117
Sentence-phrase-word, 134
Shanahan, T., 89, 102
Short recaps, 53
Sight words, 62, 69, 77, 95
Simonsmeier, B. A., 34
Single-syllable words, 151, 160, 165
Standardized Test for the Assessment of Reading
(STAR), 146
Student values, 27–28
Success and motivation, 14–15
Suffix sorts, 162–163
Syllable juncture, 63
Syllables, 63–64, 67, 70–72, 151, 160, 167
Syntax, 66, 103, 122, 168

Tai, R. H., 41
Texts, 55
accessible informational, 50, 51
complex, 164
easier-to-read, 125
regenerated, 135
rendering, 134
school, 104
sets, 50–51
synthetic, 169
The New Teacher Project (TNPT), 30
Think-aloud, 40, 129, 130, 132
Tortorelli, L., 125
Transferable background knowledge, 42–44
Tutor/tutoring, 143–144
content and instruction, 145, 150–151
effective, 145, 151
frequency and duration, 145, 149–150
identification of students, 145, 146–148
morphology and word study, 161–163
progress monitoring, 145, 151–153

Vaughn, S., 150, 152
Verbal reasoning, 169
    activate dialogue, 132–134
    description, 119–121
    GLA, 131–132
    knowledge and metacognition, 128–131
    knowledge-building, 123–125
    learning station, 138
    metacognitive thinking, 128, 139
    reading comprehension, 121–123, 125–128, 130, 139
    scaffolds, 135–139
    self-monitoring, 123
Video game market, 14–15
Vocabulary knowledge. *See* Word knowledge
Vorstius, C., 103

Wang, Z., 61
Whole class choral reading, 74–75
Withdrawing, 20
Word
    journals, 89–90
    sums, 163
    walls, 95–96
Word knowledge, 168–169
    approaches to consider, 87–88
    breadth and depth, 81
    knowledge sources, reading, 80–81
    morphological awareness in, 83–86
    multisyllabic words, 82
    new words and word phrases, 82–83

selection, words for instruction, 86–87
    vocabulary-teaching approach, 90–91
    word consciousness, 89–90
    word-learning experiences, 91–96
    word-learning strategies, 96–98
Word-learning, 81, 83
    affinity mapping, 94–95
    building academic language, routines for, 88, 92–93
    direct, 82
    hexagonal thinking, 93–94
    indirect, 82
    strategies, 96–98
    word walls, 95–96
Word recognition, 168
    building fluency, 72–73
    decoding abilities, students, 61–62, 68
    explicit instruction in, 152–157
    fluency, 64–66
    reading comprehension, 62–66, 77
    Read This to Me strategy, 73–74
    repeated and choral reading, 66–67
    strategies, 69–72
    syllables, 64, 71
    systematic instruction in, 151–152
    teacher modeling, 67
    whole class choral reading, 74–77

Young, C., 72

Zwiers, J., 133

Take your teaching further

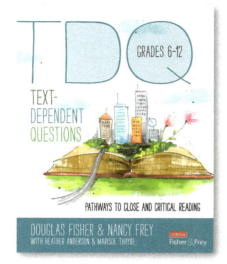
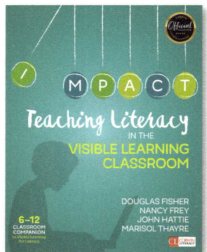
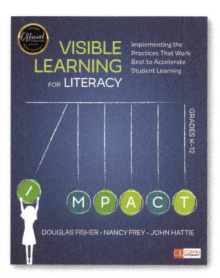
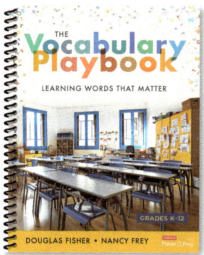
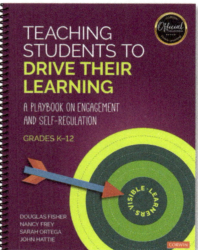

You may also be interested in...

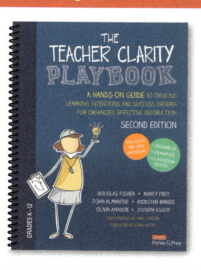
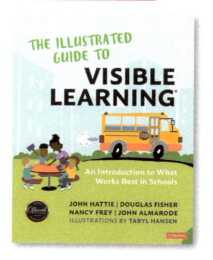
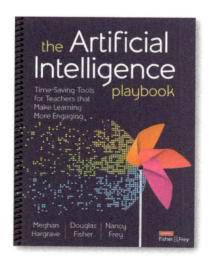

To learn more, visit **corwin.com**

Put your learning into practice

When you're ready to take your learning deeper, begin your journey with our PD services. Our personalized professional learning workshops are designed for schools or districts who want to engage in high-quality PD with a certified consultant, measure their progress, and evaluate their impact on student learning.

CORWIN Teacher Clarity

Students learn more when expectations are clear

As both a method and a mindset, Teacher Clarity allows the classroom to transform into a place where teaching is made clear. Learn how to explicitly communicate to students what they will be learning on a given day, why they're learning it, and how to know if they were successful.

Get started at corwin.com/teacherclarity

Belonging in School

Fostering Inclusion and Well-Being for Every Student

Having a sense of belonging is a prerequisite for students to bring their whole selves to learning, thereby unlocking their full potential. Belonging is more than a feeling; it's a fundamental human need. For students, feeling valued, respected, and part of a larger community significantly boosts their engagement and academic performance.

Get started at corwin.com/belonging

CORWIN Visible Learning+®

Translate the science of how we learn into practices for the classroom

Discover how learning works and how this translates into potential for enhancing and accelerating learning. Learn how to develop a shared language of learning and implement the science of learning in schools and classrooms.

Get started at corwin.com/visiblelearning

Experience the Corwin Difference.
Learn more at **corwin.com/the-corwin-difference**

CORWIN

Helping educators make the greatest impact

CORWIN HAS ONE MISSION: to enhance education through intentional professional learning.

We build long-term relationships with our authors, educators, clients, and associations who partner with us to develop and continuously improve the best evidence-based practices that establish and support lifelong learning.